MORE HOUSING, MORE FAIRLY

MORE HOUSING, MORE FAIRLY:

Report of the Twentieth Century Fund
Task Force on Affordable Housing

Background Paper on the
Limits of Privatization

By Michael A. Stegman

The Twentieth Century Fund Press/New York/1991

The Twentieth Century Fund is a research foundation undertaking timely analyses of economic, political, and social issues. Not-for-profit and non-partisan, the Fund was founded in 1919 and endowed by Edward A. Filene.

Library of Congress Cataloging-in-Publication Data

More housing, more fairly: report of the Twentieth Century Fund Task Force on Affordable Housing: background paper on the limits of privatization / by Michael A. Stegman.

   p. cm.

   Includes index.

   ISBN 0-87078-307-6 : $9.95

   1. Public housing—Government policy—United States. 2. Public housing—United States—Case studies. 3. Poor—Housing—United States. I. Stegman, Michael A. II. Twentieth Century Fund. Task Force on Affordable Housing.

HD7288.78.U5M67   1991

363.5'85'0973—dc20

91-39087

CIP

Foreword

The Twentieth Century Fund sponsors task forces in the hope that bringing together groups with diverse backgrounds and expertise will result in reports that will initiate or add to current public policy debate. The groups themselves, once constituted, have considerable sovereignty. Although they must stick to the topic, they can shape their deliberations and formulate their recommendations as they choose. The efforts of the Task Force on Affordable Housing could serve as a model for this process. Recognizing that the problem of providing housing for Americans of moderate means has been growing, the Task Force members decided early that they would be ambitious in their scope and specific in their recommendations. Although this Report may not please everyone (not even every member of the group), no one can say that this Task Force failed to come to grips with the scale of the problem and the constraints on potential solutions.

Some argue that no single housing program will make much difference and a new paradigm is needed. This conclusion is not surprising given that the work of a generation in piecing together a housing policy has been undone over the past decade. The Task Force found that federal support for housing programs, for example, had been cut by *80 percent*. For most of the same period, all-in cost of mortgages (including "points") stayed in double digits. While the mortgage interest deduction survived, lower income tax rates reduced its impact. Federal tax advantages for developers and builders of housing were drastically curtailed. And the savings and loan industry, originally intended to provide low-cost mortgage money, self-destructed. It should come as no surprise, then, that recent levels of annual housing starts are approximately the same as those at the time the nation had only a little over half our current population.

To their credit, the Task Force members took these deficiencies as challenges. The recommendations that follow are bold, including price tags and sources of funding for the programs they propose.

The Twentieth Century Fund thanks Chairman Thomas S. Johnson and the members of the Task Force for their willingness to produce so extensive and compelling a blueprint for housing policy in the United States. We also commend Michael A. Stegman, professor and chairman of the Department of City and Regional Planning of the University of North Carolina at Chapel Hill, for his background paper, "The Limits of Privatization," which laid the foundation for the group's deliberations.

When the national government, as it must, turns serious attention to the problem of housing for the nation's middle- and low-income families, *More Housing, More Fairly* surely will be a significant source of ideas and guidance for those charged with creating a new housing policy.

Richard C. Leone, PRESIDENT
The Twentieth Century Fund
November 1991

Contents

Members of the Task Force

Thomas S. Johnson, *chairman*
Former President
Manufacturers Hanover Trust Co., Inc.
New York

C. Douglas Ades
Consultant

C. Austin Fitts
The Hamilton Group, Inc.
Washington, D.C.

J. Roderick Heller, III
Chairman and CEO
National Corporation for
    Housing Partnerships
Washington, D.C.

Langley C. Keyes
Professor of City Planning
Massachusetts Institute of
    Technology

Felice Michetti
Commissioner
New York City Department of
    Housing Preservation and
    Development

Melvin A. Mister
Vice President
Clayton Brown & Associates, Inc.
New York

Earl Phillips
Director
Metropolitan Dade County
    Department of Housing
    and Urban Development
Miami

Richard Ravitch
Lawyer and Businessman
New York

David C. Schwartz
Executive Director
American Affordable Housing In-
    stitute at Rutgers University

Joseph M. Sullivan
Executive Vice President, Board
    of Trustees
Catholic Charities
Diocese of Brooklyn

Avis C. Vidal
Director
Community Development
    Research Center
New York

Louis Winnick
Senior Consultant
Fund for the City of New York

Samuel Zell
Chairman of the Board
The Equity Group
Chicago

Michael A. Stegman, *rapporteur*
Professor of City and Regional
    Planning
University of North Carolina at
    Chapel Hill

EXECUTIVE SUMMARY

The housing needs of America's poor and moderate-income families are immense and growing. While the nation spends nearly $100 billion on housing, too little of it is used to meet the needs of those who are without shelter, or who live in dilapidated homes or housing they cannot afford. The Twentieth Century Fund Task Force on Affordable Housing is realistic about the nation's financial plight. But it also recognizes that this is a wealthy nation, too often lacking the will rather than the means to address essential issues of fairness. **Our report calls for a national commitment to provide more housing, and to provide it more fairly.**

We urge the federal government to recognize that, as one of our members put it: "Affordable housing is not merely a compassionate, moral obligation of government. It is an essential ingredient of a well-functioning and secure society." To realize this goal, the Task Force proposes four basic strategies.

1. **Increase the ability of low- and moderate-income families to afford adequate housing.** The Task Force urges Congress to address the regional inequities of the patchwork-quilt public welfare system: States must raise public assistance benefits to a level that ensures access to decent housing regardless of a family's location. **The Task Force proposes pegging the shelter allocation in the welfare program to HUD-defined "fair market rents" for existing housing, at a cost of about $10 billion a year.** Housing quality standards should be attached to these funds. Rather than continuing to administer the housing portion of the public assistance program through social service agencies with little housing expertise and no inspection capabilities, the increased shelter allowance should be delivered by local housing agencies in the form of housing vouchers that can be used to rent standard housing anywhere in the local market.

1

2. **Increase the supply of affordable housing.** The Task Force recommends funding for the most critical provisions of the National Affordable Housing Act of 1990. The Task Force also recommends that Congress significantly expand the affordable housing component of the savings and loan program by taking creative advantage of the real estate now under control of the Resolution Trust Corporation (RTC). Preservation of existing units is the most efficient way to deal with the supply side of the nation's housing problem.

3. **Give public housing tenants more control over the units they live in, recognizing that wholesale privatization of public housing without unit-for-unit replacement is not a sound policy.** Even a small-scale conversion will fail without a significant investment in social services.

4. **Confront the funding needs these initiatives represent.** The nation must begin by weighing the price it pays—in terms of fewer and more costly units of new housing—against the value to society of federal laws like the Davis-Bacon Act and state and local development regulations that restrict new housing development and raise housing prices. After looking for ways to reduce the cost of housing through better management and reduction in barriers to development, we need to examine whether the current array of federal interventions reflects the nation's needs and priorities. **Reducing the primary housing tax expenditures* made by the federal government—the mortgage interest deduction and the capital gains exclusion—should provide important sources of funding for new programs without increasing net federal commitments to housing.**

---

* "Tax expenditures" refers to specific tax provisions designed to promote particular policy objectives. These include the mortgage interest deduction and capital gains exclusion on the sale of homes.

REPORT OF THE TASK FORCE

Introduction

This is a critical time in our nation's history. We are grappling with the effects of the ongoing budget crisis, the recession, the restructuring of the nation's financial system, and the changing world economy. Yet in the midst of these troubling and uncertain times, when domestic priorities run the risk of being lost in the shuffle of world events, there are urgent problems in our nation that demand, and deserve, our attention: the problems of poverty and of homelessness. We owe it to ourselves, and to those in need, not to let these problems fester and grow worse.

Forty years ago, Congress adopted the goal of a decent home in a suitable environment for every American family. For millions of Americans, this goal remains out of reach. It is a dream not only unattainable but fading rapidly in the face of the first decline in the national home-ownership rate since World War II.

From a housing standpoint, the 1980s was a decade of contrasts. Although millions of American families are better housed today than they were ten years ago, millions more are worse off, struggling just to keep a roof over their heads. Tens of thousands of Americans, including a growing number of families with young children, are without a home of any kind. And only about a third of those needing government help receive any assistance at all.

There has been progress. Public intervention in the housing markets has been an effective policy for generations of families in this country. Indeed, the federal commitment to housing remains enormous and growing when tax expenditures and credit enhancements are considered in addition to direct spending. But the bulk of federal intervention—tax expenditures for mortgage interest deductibility and a host of federal credit devices—continues to benefit upper- and middle-income homeowners at the expense of the needy.

We must help those most in need. After an inexcusable retreat from past commitments—marked by an 80 percent decline in new federal funding commitments for housing production over the past decade—the federal government has made modest steps in the past year toward recognizing its historic responsibility to help solve our nation's affordable housing problems. The recent announcement by the Federal National Mortgage Association (Fannie Mae) of $10 billion in new commitments to low- and moderate-income housing is a welcome and important step. And the enactment of the landmark, bipartisan National Affordable Housing Act of 1990 signals a renewed commitment to the federal housing goal of a decent home for every American family. But the Housing Act will be little more than cynical rhetoric unless the bill's goals are supported by sufficient federal dollars to fund its most essential provisions. (See the Appendix, pp. 19–21, for proposals.)

The housing market is in crisis. The nation is producing barely one million new units of housing a year—less than it produced forty years ago, when the population was much smaller and families were larger—and less of it is affordable to the nation's poor. There are many reasons why so few new units are produced: for one, the cost of housing has risen dramatically, in part because of government regulation. However well intended, virtually every federal, state, and local rule has increased housing costs. Higher costs have also resulted from improved quality, shrinking financing options (especially with the collapse of the savings and loan industry), and the fact that the housing industry has not achieved any dramatic productivity improvements over time. These factors and others have driven housing costs up at twice the rate of inflation. The millions of low- and moderate-income Americans whose incomes have fallen over the past decade simply cannot afford what little housing is constructed. The "trickle down" approach has not worked in this environment of increasing poverty and diminished supply.

We know America can do better. The current budget difficulties should not mask the fact that we are a very wealthy nation—a nation in which most people believe in the obligation to provide at least some minimum level of welfare for society's least fortunate members.

The Goals of the Task Force

Building on the tentative national consensus about the desired ends of national housing policy—and the growing sense of urgency to implement it—the Twentieth Century Fund brought together a diverse group of leading Americans from the private, public, and nonprofit communities to help advance the dialogue on the most appropriate means of achieving our nation's housing goals. The fourteen members have served over the year as the Twentieth Century Fund Task Force on Affordable Housing.

The Task Force's decision to emphasize means was influenced by the Bush administration's adoption of a homeownership-oriented low-income housing policy featuring the sale of public housing to tenants. Such a program, publicized by sound bites about "empowerment" and the "New Paradigm," is at best limited in its application. Indeed, some of the administration's affordable housing policies may be inimical to the very goals they claim to advance. It is critical to the success of our national housing agenda that we not allow rhetoric to substitute for action, and that attractive language does not lead us to choose means contrary to our ends.

The Task Force therefore did not revisit each of the many goals of federal housing policy, nor did we spend a great deal of time documenting a national housing problem that surrounds us daily. Instead, we sought to build upon the work done by Congress and myriad commissions, panels, and think tanks over the past decade. We focused on clearing away the rhetoric so we can begin to shape the most effective tools to achieve the goals many of us share.

The housing problems of America's neediest can only be solved by committing additional national resources. These resources need not all come from government—the private sector and the nonprofit community (including community-based organizations and labor unions) have roles to play. But we should be clear about one thing: the housing needs of this nation's poorest families cannot be met without money from somewhere. The development of ever more complex tools to hide the commitment of national resources for housing—such as the regulation of the savings and loans that obscured their real role as providers of affordable housing for millions—can lead to distortions and worse. Therefore, **the Task Force calls for an increased national commitment to the housing needs of America's low- and moderate-income families.**

Ultimately, the housing problems of our most vulnerable citizens are attributable to poverty; until the nation confronts this issue directly, no solution will be efficient or effective. Without losing sight of the overwhelming needs of our most vulnerable families, we must also develop housing strategies to deal with the needs of families of modest means—especially first-time homebuyers, those families for whom the initial down payment may be an impenetrable barrier to achieving their American dream. In this time of constrained resources, we dare not let our vision or our imaginations be constrained.

The Persistent Need for Affordable Housing

Over the past half century, there have been dramatic improvements in the quality of housing for the majority of Americans, including substantially larger homes with more amenities. But too many Americans continue to lack adequate, affordable housing. The statistics are troubling:

- In 1987, more than two-thirds of all poor families (those with incomes below the poverty line) lived in substandard housing and/or spent more than half of their incomes on housing. (Most federal and local standards assume that no more than 30 percent of family income should be consumed by housing costs.)
- While more than twice as many poor families pay unaffordable housing costs as live in substandard housing, the number of poor families living in substandard housing (2.5 million) remains unacceptably high.
- In 1987, there were 1,096,000 substandard housing units in central cities—and yet most substandard housing units were outside cities (560,000 in suburban communities and 836,000 in nonmetropolitan areas).
- A quarter of all poor renters in unsubsidized housing live in substandard units, as do nearly a third of all poor black families, more than a fifth of poor elderly, and a fifth of all single-parent families.

While the poor are far more likely than others to be inadequately housed, moderate- and middle-income families also have great difficulty securing adequate and affordable housing. In 1985, the latest year for which national data are available, nearly two million families with incomes above 80 percent of the median (4.3 percent) lived in substandard housing. Nearly five million families (11.6 percent) paid more than 30 percent of their income for housing. The problem is worse for middle-income renters than for middle-income homeowners: for renters, the incidence of substandard housing is nearly twice as great and the incidence of excessive housing outlays is nearly three times greater than for moderate-income homeowners.

Current Federal Housing and Welfare Assistance Programs
In recent years, federal housing aid for the poor has favored rental assistance over support for housing production. As a result, the line between housing and welfare (income maintenance) programs has blurred. The percentage of poor households receiving both housing and welfare benefits nearly doubled between 1974 and 1987 and is growing rapidly.

Despite some modest gains, federal intervention in the housing market for low-income families has been inadequate to address the need.

The problem does not lie in the administration of public assistance programs. While underreporting of income, mismanagement, and even fraud are occasionally uncovered in these programs, even much improved management could not alter the fact that our national housing and public assistance programs are dwarfed by the needs of those with low and moderate incomes. The mere existence of substantial housing problems in areas that have experienced housing surpluses—and there are many—demonstrates that current household incomes cannot absorb the supply. And in those areas of the country with housing shortages—especially high-cost big cities—weaknesses in demand due to low incomes are exacerbated by supply shortfalls, driving up prices and turning the American dream into a pipe dream for many.

Federal Housing Efforts Today: The $100 Billion Pot

The real measure of federal commitment to housing includes not only direct expenditures but also the benefits extended through federal tax expenditures. Including administrative costs, federal housing efforts total nearly $100 billion a year.

Direct Federal Spending. During the 1980s, the federal government's commitment to low-income housing went into full-scale retreat. New budget authority (congressional approval of program initiatives) for low-income housing—specifically, multiyear commitments for new subsidized housing units—plummeted 75 percent, from nearly $41 billion to an estimated $10 billion in real terms. The number of subsidized housing starts per year dropped by more than 88 percent—from 175,000 to less than 21,000.

Some have argued that the systematic decline in new annual budget authority during the 1980s was the result of a growing federal preference for rental assistance over new construction, not a reduced federal commitment to housing. Because new construction requires longer-term subsidy contracts—and therefore higher amounts of budget authority—than do commitments for rental assistance, it is possible that the switchover could account for some of the reduction in new budget authority without causing a proportionate decline in the number of households receiving assistance. Proponents of this argument cite a steady rise in the number of households receiving housing subsidies (approximately one million more in 1988 than in 1979) and a corresponding increase in total annual outlays for assisted housing (more than doubling in real terms, from $8.9 billion to $17.3 billion).

The fact is, however, that the federal government's move toward rental assistance (with a concomitant reduction in new budget authority) has been accompanied by a reduction in the number of newly assisted households each year. Concurrent with the federal government's virtual elimination of all new low-income construction programs—which, just ten years ago, supported more than 125,000 new housing units—net additions to the rental assistance/voucher rolls averaged fewer than 84,000 households per year between fiscal 1979 and 1990. The early legacy of the Bush/Kemp administration continues the trend: there were only 57,000 newly assisted households in fiscal years 1990 and 1991.

Despite the alleged cost-effectiveness of vouchers over new construction, greater efficiency has not been achieved. The administration has neither managed to maintain the same number of new households receiving assistance each year at a lower cost nor managed to help more households at the same cost. Instead, there has been a substantial decline in new federal commitments to low-income housing of all kinds.

Federal Tax Expenditures. When tax treatment is considered, it is clear that the poorest members of our society have not been getting a fair share of the federal housing subsidies that Congress has made available. For example, the amount of money spent on all low-income subsidized housing programs in fiscal year 1989 ($17.3 billion) was slightly more than a quarter of the total amount of federal tax expenditures for all homeowners ($63 billion) and about half as much as the value of the tax break associated with the deductibility of mortgage interest ($34.2 billion).

Tax benefits to homeowners are rarely viewed as subsidies—in direct contrast to low-income housing assistance—and as such do not carry the stigma often associated with the subsidies that go to public and assisted housing. Yet these tax expenditures reflect just as important a policy decision as the more explicit and visible direct federal expenditures.

Further, the $54 billion in federal tax expenditures for homeowners favor the most affluent. In 1988, for example, two-thirds of these benefits went to households with incomes of $50,000 or more. When low-income housing outlays and housing tax expenditures are combined, households with incomes of $50,000 or more received 52.2 percent of the benefits of federal housing efforts.

Even before tax reform, the tax code favored investment in homeownership over rental housing, which is the primary form of housing for low-income families. The Tax Reform Act did nothing to reverse this situation. In fiscal year 1989, for example, federal tax expenditures for rental housing ($8.5 billion) were only a sixth as large as for owner-occupied housing—even though there are over 33 million rental units in this country. In fact, the federal bias against investment in new rental housing has been substantially increased through the Tax Reform Act, which reduces depreciation allowances, increases capital gains tax rates, and imposes new passive income rules that make it more difficult to use tax losses on real estate to offset income from other sources. In the long run, as these changes in the tax system work their way through local housing markets, the Tax Reform Act will reduce the value of the federal tax subsidy to the average renter by more than 50 percent.

Recommendations

This Task Force endorses four strategies for providing more—and more fairly distributed—housing. The first is aimed at helping low- and moderate-income families afford the housing they need. The second is intended to increase the housing supply. The third is geared toward promoting tenant self-sufficiency. The fourth endorses a funding strategy that promotes fairness and fiscal prudence.

The Task Force recognizes that the crucial demand- and supply-side strategies are the responsibility of the federal government. Federal efforts to "devolve" functions to subnational governments force states and localities to raise taxes, which are often harmful to their economic well-being and often result in the least equitable distribution of costs and services. Any program that has substantial distributional effects must take place at the highest level of government, or risk causing people to "vote with their feet" by leaving higher-tax jurisdictions.

Strategy One: Help Low- and Moderate-Income
Families Afford Adequate Housing

In much of the nation, the problem is not that there is too little housing, but rather that there are too many families with too little income to afford the housing already available. Certainly there are severe housing shortages in some areas. National approaches should recognize regional housing market differences, and strategies should be developed to reflect those variations. But in virtually all parts of the nation, inadequate incomes are at the root of the housing crisis.

Increase the Shelter Grant. To deal with this problem, the Task Force urges the federal government to recognize the linkages between welfare and housing assistance programs. Both programs must be adjusted to reflect the costs of securing decent and safe housing for the most vulnerable families. Failure to do so has resulted in an unprecedented number of public assistance families using their basic welfare allowances to pay for often inadequate housing. The nation's housing programs are too poorly funded to compensate for the failures of the public assistance system. In order to address the inequities that have come to characterize the patchwork-quilt public welfare system, **the Task Force recommends that Congress require states to raise public assistance benefits to a level that ensures access to decent housing regardless of a family's location.**

The Task Force proposes pegging the shelter allocation in the welfare program to HUD-defined "fair market rents" for existing housing. And in order to stop the flow of scarce federal dollars into slum housing markets, housing quality standards should be attached to the public assistance program.

Pegging AFDC shelter allocations to HUD's "fair market rents" would cost about $10 billion a year. But the budget impact would be much less because this reform would eliminate the piggybacking of housing and welfare subsidies for the same families. It would also reduce the operating deficits of local public housing authorities. The reason for this is that public housing authorities may not charge public assistance families more than the maximum shelter allocation in rent, even though the costs of operating housing units are often much higher. Lower public housing authority operating deficits would translate into lower federal public housing operating subsidies.

The Task Force believes that the housing portion of the public assistance program should no longer be administered by state social service agencies, which have little housing expertise and no inspection capabilities. **The Task Force recommends that the increased shelter allowance be delivered instead by local public housing authorities in the form of vouchers to be used to rent standard housing anywhere in the local market.** This would simply be an expansion of the housing voucher program already administered by local public housing authorities.

The Task Force recognizes that the transfer of the housing responsibilities of the public assistance system to local public housing authorities will require new administrative arrangements at the local level that are not without cost and inconvenience. But the Task Force is convinced that the costs would be far smaller than those of initiating a housing capability within local public assistance programs. Without such a transfer of responsibility, the Task Force would not make this proposal a centerpiece of its recommended housing strategy.

The Task Force also believes that the federal government must rationalize its funding formulas. Although the federal government pays just 50 percent of the AFDC program (the other half is paid by states and localities), it currently pays the full cost of the housing voucher program. **The Task force recommends that the full incremental cost of the increase in shelter allocations (in the form of an expanded housing voucher program) be borne by the federal government.**

Strategy Two: Increase the Supply of Housing

The Task Force recommends several approaches for dealing with the shortage of affordable housing. First, we must remove barriers to the construction of new low-cost housing. This includes reforming construction and building-code standards that are outdated or simply protective of certain industries, and revising restrictive local zoning codes. Further, states and localities should identify and resolve local barriers to the use of lower-cost construction techniques and land-use formulas.

The public sector cannot solve the housing problem without significant involvement on the part of the private sector. We must find new ways to bring more private-sector capital into the housing market. We should consider incentives for employer-assisted housing—such as those recently announced by Fannie Mae—and encourage unions to help develop housing for members. Pension funds are an enormous potential source of capital for new construction and renovation; relatively minor changes in the ERISA provisions that regulate pension fund investment, currently under consideration by the Department of Labor, could make a valuable contribution.

Because the federal government has a poor record of managing new construction programs (its size and distance from America's communities make these failures understandable, even predictable), the Task Force believes that new development programs should be implemented at the local level. In recognition of the nation's diversity of needs and opportunities, and to encourage local creativity, the federal government should direct all new construction efforts through the states and localities, and merge as many development programs as possible into block grants. These block grants should not serve as a prelude to reduced federal commitments. Rather, the federal government should make every effort to ensure that the states and localities use the new block grants to address the areas of greatest need, not those of least resistance.

The tools chosen to deal with the housing supply problem should be those that least distort the economic decisions of families and businesses. Tax incentives and other tools that offer hidden benefits may have unpredictable results; regulatory approaches may have even worse effects over the long term. The Task Force believes the best way to proceed is with simple and open redistributive tools that increase the resources available to those with low and moderate incomes.

Fund Key Provisions of the National Affordable Housing Act of 1990. The federal government struggled hard to come to agreement over the recently passed National Affordable Housing Act of 1990. Yet the bill is languishing as an authorization without appropriation. Given the enormity of the needs we face and the importance of prompt action,

the Task Force recommends funding for the most critical provisions of the National Affordable Housing Act of 1990. This means focusing the nation's limited resources on the housing programs we know can work efficiently, rather than experimenting with new and untested initiatives (such as the HOPE program, which holds little promise of success). The costs of such targeted funding will be much less than the $4 billion estimated for the entire bill, and will serve as a down payment on meeting the nation's enormous housing needs.

Protect the Existing Housing Supply. The least costly way to increase the availability of housing for low- and moderate-income families is to prevent the diminution of the existing supply. Federal programs should be aimed at shoring up (physically and financially) the most vulnerable units—especially those in federal programs such as 236 and 221(d)3, where current subsidies may soon run out. The loss of these units from the affordable housing stock would be a tragic irony when their replacement may cost so much more.

The assisted-housing stock suffers from a plague of shortsighted regulations and policies. As a result, private-sector housing developers, especially those that are well managed, are reducing their participation, and the better state and local agencies, as well as nonprofits, are not as interested as we need them to be. Further, ill-considered Section 8 funding and workout policies are substantially increasing the present value cost of the distressed portion of this stock.

The Task Force recommends that Congress significantly expand the affordable housing component of the savings and loan bailout by taking creative advantage of the real estate now under control of the Resolution Trust Corporation. There are numerous tools that have been proposed to accomplish this end, and the Task Force supports a multi-faceted approach.

For example, the National Housing Partnership proposes the creation of a nonprofit foundation that would acquire existing multifamily rental properties from the Resolution Trust Corporation at market value for rental to low-, moderate-, and middle-income families. The benefits of such a program are many: it is a cost-effective means of expanding the affordable rental supply; it avoids dumping apartment projects in already depressed real estate markets (thereby avoiding endangering additional depository institutions); it provides cash to the Resolution Trust Corporation and reduces the budgetary impact of the bailout; and it relieves the government of responsibility for managing residential housing, an area in which much of the public sector has little experience or capability. Putting these properties in the hands of competent professional management will enhance value.

Strengthen the Rental Housing Component of the Housing Program.
HUD's emphasis on extending homeownership opportunities to lower-income families may prove a useful adjustment to our national housing policy. So, too, may HUD's intention to fine-tune all rental assistance programs to promote resident self-sufficiency and opportunities to move out of public and assisted housing. Within this policy framework, it would also be appropriate to change federal law to authorize the use of housing vouchers to help low-income families buy homes and to expand the use of Section 8 rental certificates to promote homeownership (their use is currently restricted to co-ops).

But the Task Force believes that it would be inappropriate to limit the homeownership-enhancing benefits of these subsidies to public housing homeownership schemes—which is what HUD proposes to do. Paying too large a share of income for housing has become the most widespread housing problem in the country. Whether applied to rentals or home-ownership, there are far too few vouchers and certificates in circulation. Rather than making privatization initiatives the centerpiece of a revitalized national housing policy, **the Task Force recommends a major expansion of rental housing assistance and supply.**

Despite the urgent need for significant expansion of our rental assistance programs, President Bush's proposed fiscal year 1992 housing budget calls for an incremental allocation of less than 80,000 housing vouchers. The Task Force recommends that this total be increased substantially. An increase to 200,000 new vouchers is not out of line; the incremental net cost (over the currently funded 80,000 vouchers) would be $700 million in fiscal year 1992 outlays and $3.5 billion in budget authority.

Strategy Three: Promote Tenant Self-Sufficiency

The Task Force recognizes the need to increase tenants' control over their lives, their housing, and their communities. At the same time, the Task Force is deeply skeptical of programs that imply that such control can substitute for the very real financial resources families need to maintain their housing.

Debate within as well as outside the Bush administration has focused on the development of a new policy approach, sometimes labeled the "New Paradigm." This approach is based on the notion of "empowerment"—that is, giving poor people, who are currently the objects of vast and sometimes paternalistic federal policies, greater authority over their lives. Although not then called a "New Paradigm," this was an important theme in the president's most recent State of the Union address; its notions of choice, community control, and individual decisionmaking are attractive to a broad range of Americans.

In some respects, the New Paradigm is a welcome advance over the prior administration's domestic policy. It acknowledges that the government must confront urgent social problems. The administration's market-oriented approach is also compatible with the public's desire to solve problems without increasing taxes or expanding government payrolls. But it is clear to the Task Force that whatever the strengths of this approach, it is no substitute for a meaningful commitment to affordable housing.

Recognize the Limits of Privatizing Public Housing. The Task Force believes that privatizing public housing is very costly, is very hard to do right, and has very limited application. Further, by providing large benefits to a few (it could cost $70,000 to $90,000 per new homeowner) while leaving most of the poor unserved, privatization is not only expensive but inequitable.

By disproportionately channeling federal funds for support services and modernization to resident-managed projects slated for sale, privatization discriminates against public housing families who happen not to be living in one of the relatively few resident-managed projects. Focusing management reforms on the handful of resident-managed developments fails to deal with systemic problems that discourage work effort, divorce housing quality from rental price, and create severe concentrations of desperately poor families.

The case for privatizing public housing is based in large part on the benefits that accrue from decentralizing decisionmaking and accountability to the project level. But the Task Force found no evidence that resident management organizations are any more democratic, efficient, or accountable than well-performing public housing authorities.

The Task Force believes that no privatization effort should be undertaken without a clear commitment that every unit lost to the public housing stock will be replaced on a unit-for-unit basis.

Enhance Support Services for Resident Management Initiatives. The Task Force believes that HUD's emphasis on resident initiatives in managing public housing is a valuable addition to public housing policies. But HUD should not embrace resident management as the sole, or even primary, route to public housing reform in the 1990s. Some of the newest and most exciting programs place the same emphasis on self-sufficiency using different methods: strengthening the family unit; teaching job skills that enable a family to move out of public housing into a homeownership situation; using revenues raised through sale of public housing to create additional homeownership opportunities; ridding housing developments of the scourge of drugs.

The Task Force believes that unless there is adequate training and support for the families involved, tenant management programs will fail. Specialized human-capital development programs must be designed and implemented to help public housing tenants take over functions that others have performed for them, thus decreasing their dependency and increasing their sense of control.

The Task Force recognizes that social services are critical to any tenant management effort. In fact, they are the key to effective implementation of any housing strategy for the poor and others who suffer from multiple social dysfunctions. Housing is a start, but it cannot be the end of any meaningful program of empowerment.

Strategy Four: Confront the Funding Needs

If the nation is to deal with its housing problems, it must begin by rebuilding the consensus that, in a society as rich as ours, some minimum level of welfare should be provided to all members and that housing is a part of such a social contract. The United States can afford more assistance to its most vulnerable. What we lack is the will, not the means. Given the importance of housing in nurturing family life, creating vital communities, and stimulating the economy, the United States cannot afford to continue spending less than one penny out of every federal dollar on housing.

The Task Force recognizes that none of its proposed reforms is without cost. Our recommendations would lead to new federal spending of as much as $15 billion a year, phased in over the next few years. But the Task Force is also aware of the federal government's fiscal problems, and those of the 80,000 other jurisdictions in this country. So we propose to deal with housing financing in two ways: First, over the long term, **the Task Force calls for increased investment in housing by the public and private sectors in this nation.** We will be a stronger and more just nation for making such a commitment. Second, **if fiscal constraints or political realities delay increased investment, the Task Force calls for greater efficiency in existing programs and the reallocation of federal funding to support the initiatives we have recommended.** This does not mean the Task Force is satisfied that current commitment levels are adequate, but only that until funding is used as efficiently and as fairly as possible, the case for increased spending will be weak.

Make Housing Dollars Go Further. The Task Force recognizes that public policy involves managing competing goals. In the case of housing, competing goals often result in reduced housing production and higher costs. As a result of burdensome federal regulations, for example, builders often avoid participation in Federal Housing Administration (FHA) programs. State and local building codes and local zoning laws increase housing costs beyond what most can afford. It may be useful to allocate federal dollars to encourage removal of state and local barriers to efficient housing construction.

The Task Force recommends streamlining federal, state, and local housing standards and programs. It also recommends that labor laws, such as the Davis-Bacon Act, which add to the cost of building new housing without benefiting those in need, should be redesigned or eliminated.

Manage Existing Programs Better. The next place to look for resources to reallocate to the housing initiatives we have recommended is improved productivity in managing programs already in place. The myriad federal housing programs can be run more efficiently and effectively. Any dollars made available as a result should be redirected toward expansion of the most efficient housing programs. The administration has shown that it understands the importance of good management at HUD—this commitment should be sought for all federal housing agencies. The FHA should be reestablished as an off-budget independent agency to serve that part of the mortgage credit market not being served by the Federal Home Loan Mortgage Corporation (Freddie Mac), Fannie Mae, and other for-profit entities. In addition, the Task Force has appended to this report a list of possible changes in HUD and FHA programs to illustrate the kinds of improvements in housing program management that the federal government should pursue.

Shift Federal Commitments to Make Current Allocations Fair. The federal commitment to housing is nearly $100 billion in direct and tax expenditures. But does the current array of federal interventions reflect the nation's needs and priorities? The Task Force believes that the time has come for some redirection of federal efforts toward a rebuilding of America.

The Task Force believes the nation can accomplish such a reallocation of federal commitments in a number of ways. None of them will be popular, since someone will have to pay if we are to address the needs of the poor and near-poor without increasing the federal budget deficit.

Reducing two of the largest tax expenditures made by the federal government can provide significant sources of funding for new programs without increasing net federal commitments. Specifically, capping the mortgage interest deduction for all taxpayers at the 15 percent bracket (rather than allowing it to be worth 31 percent for wealthier families and 15 percent for poorer ones) would raise $15 billion a year—affecting only the wealthiest 2 percent of all households—and taxing 30 percent of capital gains from the sale of housing would yield $10 billion a year. These are essential tools for reallocating existing federal subsidies toward those who need them most.

Appendix
PROPOSALS TO IMPROVE THE EFFECTIVENESS OF FEDERAL HOUSING PROGRAMS

The Task Force believes that new initiatives should be funded first by improving the effectiveness of existing housing programs. Both the FHA and HUD should be examined closely for ways to increase the productivity of their current operations. HUD Secretary Kemp has already demonstrated a commitment to just this kind of scrutiny, and we encourage progress in this direction. Below, we have listed some of the specific proposals brought to the attention of the Task Force. Without necessarily endorsing every one, we believe they are indicative of the kinds of creative efforts that committed management teams at these agencies can implement.

Improve the Operations of HUD

Program Consolidation. Many of the remaining HUD programs should be consolidated and made more "user-friendly." The majority of them, outside of those dealing directly with maintenance of public housing, could be included in a program of block grants/tenant-based assistance provided to state and local governments and related agencies, primarily on a formula basis. The regulations related to these programs should be simplified so that (1) state and local governments have maximum flexibility to use funds as they see fit so long as they benefit those with low incomes; (2) assistance can be combined easily with other federal, state, or local support; (3) tenant-based assistance is made more flexible, portable, and dependable so that it can be used for down payments and debt service by first-time homebuyers; and

(4) priority is given to state and local governments that provide complementary services (day care, job training, etc.).

Blanket Waivers. Blanket waivers should be developed so that federal housing funds can be transferred between categories within regions pursuant to approved plans. For example, money appropriated for public housing rehabilitation could be used to purchase RTC or FHA single-family inventory for public housing tenants in areas where this method would provide housing at a lower per unit cost.

HUD Reorganization. HUD should be reorganized to increase its operating efficiency. Among the approaches that should be examined are: establishing a bureau system (like most other federal agencies), reducing the overall size of the department and the number of political Senior Executive Service positions, delegating more of the work load to the regions outside of high-cost areas, improving technical skills, and expanding automation.

Improve the Operations of the FHA

In addition to reestablishing FHA as an off-budget independent agency to serve that part of the mortgage-credit market not being served by Freddie Mac, Fannie Mae, or other for-profit entities, the following actions should be considered.

Upgrade Single-Family Insurance Programs. The direct endorsement system should be upgraded to lower the expense of delivery and to phase in pool distribution with state and local Housing Finance Agencies (HFAs), Freddie Mac, Fannie Mae, the large private mortgage insurers (PMIs), and mortgage brokers. The emphasis in these ventures should be on affordable housing. The 1991 changes in Mutual Mortgage Insurance premiums and terms should be revised to soften the impact on first-time homebuyers. A large lease-purchase program should be introduced in response to the need for a zero percent down payment program for creditworthy families. Counseling grants should be increased from $3 million to $30 million over a three-year period; this assistance would lower default losses by at least the amount of the increase.

Create New Multifamily Insurance Programs. Joint ventures should be established with state and local HFAs, Freddie Mac, and Fannie Mae to reinsure eligible policies in affordable areas. A joint venture with the Resolution Trust Corporation should be established to provide seller financing on sales under the affordable housing program.

Use the Community Reinvestment Act as a Positive Incentive. Some of the above-mentioned initiatives can be developed for investment by financial institutions on a shared-risk basis to satisfy Community Reinvestment Act requirements. Eligibility could be ensured with the

Office of the Comptroller of the Currency (OCC) and the Federal Reserve.

Increase Technical Assistance Grants. Technical assistance grants can be substantially increased so that nonprofits and government developers can teach low-income-housing participants how to combine federal, state, local, nonprofit, and private-sector funding and financing to produce and maintain affordable housing. Currently, the complexity of the process is a major barrier to entry.

Production Financing. By working with the Federal Housing Finance Board (FHFB), Freddie Mac, and Fannie Mae, a mechanism can be developed by FHA to provide reasonable and prudent liquidity to the low-income housing market—particularly for the smaller producers who, despite good track records and highly efficient operations, have great difficulty accessing the national markets. Perhaps a partial FHA credit enhancement could be worked out for this purpose.

Improve the Information Infrastructure. As the financial system restructures itself, it is clear that increased institutional investment (pension funds, mutual funds, etc.) will be desirable in residential real estate. One of the barriers to this transformation is relatively poor disclosure on the performance of various markets. The multifamily market is a good example of this "externality." FHA is the logical candidate to provide leadership and funding for research and disclosure on performance in all areas of the residential markets.

Increase FHA Leadership in Making Affordable Housing Available. The FHA should take the lead in activities designed to make affordable housing available to those in need. Specifically, the FHA should discourage discrimination in the mortgage markets, work with the Department of the Treasury to ensure that banking legislation and regulation are not unreasonably detrimental to housing, convince institutional investors in the private markets of the benefits of investing in residential housing, and persuade the housing community that such investments will require higher standards of disclosure and professionalism.

Improve Agency Operations. The FHA bureaucracy should be reduced. There should be fewer people at higher grade levels, backed by more automated systems and outside support (contracts). In addition, more work should be delegated to regional locations, away from high-cost areas. Finally, more resources should be transferred to multifamily management and property disposition, to prevent the growing losses in this area. Financial reforms and the extension of automation, recently slowed or stopped, should be given a high priority. Technical skills should be substantially upgraded at every level.

THE LIMITS OF PRIVATIZATION

Background Paper by

Michael A. Stegman

Chapter 1
THE REAGAN/BUSH RECORD

D uring the Reagan administration, the federal government's commitment to low-income housing went into retreat.[1] New budget authority for low-income housing—multiyear commitments for additional subsidized housing—plummeted 59 percent, from nearly $25 billion to an estimated $10 billion (see Table 1). And even these drastically reduced levels of funding consistently exceeded budget requests from the Department of Housing and Urban Development (HUD). Further, consistent with the administration's favoring of rental assistance over new construction programs, the number of subsidized housing starts per year dropped by more than 88 percent, from 175,000 to less than 21,000 (see Table 2). Concurrently, the number of low-income households newly receiving federal housing assistance declined each year.

There are those who argue that housing continued to receive its fair share of federal resources under Reagan. Citing different budget statistics, they point to a steady rise in the number of households receiving housing subsidies (approximately one million more in 1988 than in 1979), and a corresponding increase in total annual federal expenditures for assisted housing (nearly tripling, from $4.3 billion to more than $16 billion).

In a December 1988 op-ed piece in the *Wall Street Journal*, economist Edgar Olsen attempted to lay to rest what he called the "persistent falsehood" that the Reagan administration contributed to the rise in homelessness by starving the low-income housing sector. Although new annual budget authority plunged over the Reagan years, Olsen argued that this was the result of an increasing federal preference for rental assistance, not due to a reduced federal commitment to housing. The switchover itself, from new construction to rental assistance, he explained, accounted for the dramatic reduction in new budget authority. Total outlays, he claimed, rose steadily.

Table 1
Budget Authority and Outlays for Subsidized Housing, 1979–90
($ million)

Fiscal Year	Budget Authority	Percent Change	Low-Income Housing Outlays	Percent Change
1979	$24,780	—	$4,367	—
1980	$27,932	+12.7	$5,632	+29.0
1981	$26,927	-3.6	$7,752	+37.6
1892	$14,608	-45.7	$8,738	+12.7
1983	$10,498	-28.1	$9,998	+14.4
1984	$12,671	+20.7	$11,270	+12.7
1985	$26,879	+112.1	$25,263	+124.2
1986	$11,643	-56.7	$12,383	-51.0
1987	$9,864	-18.0	$12,656	+2.2
1988	$9,698	-1.7	$13,906	+9.9
1989 (est)	$9,963	+2.7	$15,299	+10.0
1990 (est)	$10,207	+2.4	$16,197	+5.9
Percent Change 1979–90		-58.8		+270.9

Source: Special Memorandum, Low Income Housing Information Service, March 1989, Table 7.

Table 2
HUD-Subsidized Housing Starts and Completions, 1979–90

Year	Section 8	Public Housing	Total Starts	Percent Change
1979	153,251	21,868	175,119	—
1980	132,721	40,528	173,249	-1.1
1981	60,428	45,607	106,035	-38.8
1982	87,831	25,100	112,931	+6.5
1983	42,573	27,060	69,633	-38.3
1984	17,646	22,443	40,089	-42.4
1985	9,238	11,133	20,371	-49.2
1986	8,410	6,385	14,795	-28.9
1987	6,383	5,861	12,244	-17.2
1988	5,301	4,679	9,980	-18.5
1989 (est)	13,000	7,688	20,688	+107.3
1990 (est)	13,000	7,609	20,609	-3.8
Total	549,782	225,961	775,743	—
Percent Change 1979–90				-88.2

Source: Special Memorandum, Low Income Housing Information Service, March 1989, Table 3.

In theory, Olsen is correct. But in fact, the movement away from new construction in favor of rental assistance diminished the number of newly assisted households each year. Concurrent with the federal government's virtual elimination of all new low-income construction programs—which, just ten years ago, supported more than 125,000 new housing units—net additions to the rental assistance/voucher rolls averaged fewer than 84,000 households per year between fiscal 1979 and 1990 (see Table 3). And the first Bush/Kemp housing budget provides for a net increase of less than 50,000 vouchers and certificates for fiscal 1991.

Despite the alleged cost-effectiveness of vouchers over new construction, recent housing policy has not managed to maintain the number of new households receiving assistance each year at a lower cost. Nor has it permitted substantially more households to be helped. Rather than greater efficiency, the policy legacy of the Reagan era is a substantial decline in new federal commitments to low-income housing of any kind.

Table 3
Section 8 Housing Certificates and Housing Vouchers, 1979–90

Year	Section 8 Certificate	Housing Vouchers	Total	Percent Change
1979	107,025	0	107,025	—
1980	107,288	0	107,288	+0.3
1981	62,324	0	62,324	-41.9
1982	96,408	0	96,408	+54.7
1983	108,955	0	108,955	+13.0
1984	77,625	0	77,625	-28.8
1985	58,251	11,063	69,314	-10.7
1986	65,013	39,625	104,638	+51.0
1987	45,341	69,836	115,177	+10.1
1988	3,713	62,915	66,628	-42.2
1989	18,765	46,694	65,459	-1.8
1990 (est)	30,523	23,072	53,595	-18.1
1991 (est)	6,889	43,038	49,927	—
Total	764,143	253,539	1,084,363	
Percent Change 1979–90				-53.3

Source: Special Memorandum, Low Income Housing Information Service, March 1989, Table 3, and Fiscal 1991 HUD Budget Tables, Table 5.

The Bush administration has spoken of major budget increases for low-income housing and a strong commitment to privatization.[2] Its revitalized national housing policy would revolve around home-ownership, and be targeted at the 37 percent of Americans who are renters: "The American Dream is to own a home. The strength of the country is that we are not a nation of landless peasants, but a nation of homeowners. The man on the street needs a simple concept to grasp onto, and it should not be 'reform.' It should be 'home.' Every initiative will be designed to enhance the possibility of homeownership, even the rental assistance programs."[3] The sale of public and other federally assisted housing will be the centerpiece of the expansion of homeownership opportunities.

In fact, as we enter the second year of the Bush administration, there is not much to distinguish between the Reagan and Bush housing records. The first Bush budget for housing proposes a meager $28 million increase in outlays over a year ago. (The president proposes to spend around three-quarters of a billion dollars to privatize public housing over the next three years.) Though the new policy centers on expanding homeownership opportunities, it would extend housing assistance to "a total of only 82,049 new households, the same number on average that were committed during the Reagan years."[4]

Chapter 2
HOMEOWNERSHIP AND PRIVATIZATION

The Ideal of Homeownership

Despite a recent downturn in homeownership—the first dip in forty years, from nearly 66 percent to 63.9 percent—the United States remains largely a nation of homeowners.[1] This is no accident. Beginning with the Homestead Act more than one hundred years ago, and augmented in 1913 by federal tax incentives (costing the government more than $50 billion in 1988 alone), the U.S. government has fostered and supported the ideal of home-ownership.[2] Support has come from the highest levels of government and from both sides of the political aisle: In 1927, President Herbert Hoover declared that "a family that owns its own home takes pride in it and has a more wholesome, healthful, and happy atmosphere in which to bring up children. . . ."[3] President Franklin D. Roosevelt stated that "a nation of homeowners is unconquerable. . . ."[4] President Lyndon B. Johnson said that "owning a home can increase responsibility and stake out a man's place in his community. . . . The man who owns a home has something to be proud of and reason to protect and preserve it."[5] President Ronald Reagan said that "it [homeownership] supplies stability and rootedness."[6] As a presidential candidate, George Bush stated that "homeownership continues to be one of the highest social priorities in America."[7]

This presidential support for widespread homeownership reflects the extraordinary degree to which Americans equate having a home of their own with "having it made" and an overall sense of well-being. In the *1978 HUD Survey on the Quality of Community Life,* Louis Harris Associates reported that regardless of their present housing circumstances, 75 percent of all Americans would prefer to own a single-family house. This was true for rich and poor; white, black, and Hispanic; and families in all-white, racially mixed, or all-minority neighborhoods.[8]

Homeownership implies a degree of financial and psychological security that is not normally associated with rental occupancy. For most of the past forty years, homeownership has not only been a symbol of wealth, but also the most important actual wealth most American families accumulated. As Irving Welfeld, a HUD policy analyst, put it: "During the post-war period . . . young couples with almost no money to their name bought houses with a minimal down payment, and over the years, with the steady buildup of equity and a little inflation, before they knew it they were rich. The value of owner-occupied homes at the end of 1986 was $3.758 trillion and the net equity was $2.113 trillion—an average owner had an equity of over $50,000."[9] According to Wallace F. Smith, a noted housing scholar, "ownership is an extension of . . . privacy, for the homeowning household can be confident that its dwelling will not be entered by others except by invitation and that the family will not be required to surrender the dwelling to others."[10]

Homeownership breaks the chains of dependency between tenants and landlords. It enables families to accumulate equity, to keep pace with inflation, and to pass something on to their children. Further, government action, such as code enforcement or urban revitalization, is less likely to cause the displacement of owner-occupants than it is to force renters to find alternative accommodations. In short, the common understanding is that, all other things equal, homeowners are better off than renters because they are homeowners.

In addition to facilitating wealth creation and inducing a greater sense of psychological security among individual families, it is also argued that homeownership produces broad, societal gains. For one thing, Raymond J. Struyk, a former HUD official and policy analyst at the Urban Institute, states that homeowners save at a higher rate than renters—allowing for a higher rate of national investment and greater economic growth. In addition, homeowners maintain their dwellings in superior condition, potentially extending the life of the housing stock. Further, homeowners are more active in their local communities and, in this sense, are better citizens than renters.[11] To the extent that a higher voting rate in local and federal elections is a reasonable proxy for good citizenship, Struyk confirms a positive relationship between homeownership and citizen participation.

The Downside of Homeownership

Acceptance of the social value of homeownership is so wide-spread that there is little high-level government support for more research in the area. Nevertheless, for nearly a generation, scholars have argued a contrary view. Some of the earliest critics, like social scientist John P. Dean, believe that homeownership probably works well for middle-income families but not for working-class families.[12] In 1951, Catherine Bauer, a noted city planner, questioned whether the near-universal preference for living in single-family housing was being misinterpreted as a desire to own such housing.[13] Bauer also suggested that the traditional arguments favoring homeownership—such as security and independence, personal responsibility, family pride and status, and civic participation—might no longer be valid under present conditions, "so unlike the frontier conditions which prevailed when these values were first attached to it. Buying a more or less standard product on a small lot with little or no cash invest-ment, and with small likelihood of remaining there for more than a few years, is not the same thing as nailing together a homestead on a quarter-section of prairie."[14]

Some thirty years later, housing policy analyst Eric Carlson argues that the social costs of national homeownership policies are substan-tially understated because they fail to take into account "the provision and maintenance of infrastructure facilities and services over enormous areas; the devaluation of many inner cities; the increasing length of the journey between work and home, with accompanying traffic congestion and pollution problems; the reduction of employment mobility, as between cities and regions; and, of course, the social isolation of typical suburban life, tied to the shopping center, but cut off from the rest of the world by lawns and freeways."[15] Homeownership is also alleged to reduce residential and job market opportunities by tying workers to their current places of residence (especially when the economy is soft and selling a house is more difficult), diminishing their ability to go after better jobs in locations with stronger economies.[16]

Struyk also suggests that, out of a desire to protect their investments, homeowners could be a destabilizing force in neighborhoods under-going transitions that the homeowners perceive as declines: "The owner-occupant, as investor, may move early from transitional areas to protect an investment which often constitutes the bulk of a home-owner's wealth."[17]

These criticisms notwithstanding, the Bush administration is committed to a homeownership-centered, low-income housing policy that would help public housing tenants to buy their apartments and whole projects because "owning something changes behavior in ways that no amount of preaching middle-class values ever could."[18] In embracing public housing homeownership, Bush has bought into the proposition espoused by HUD Secretary Jack Kemp that democracy can't work without the component that goes to the heart of what freedom is all about—the chance to own a piece of property. As to how the government might help, the preferred avenue seems to be privatization.

The Foundations of Privatization

In *Privatism and Urban Policy in Britain and the United States,* Timothy Barenkov uses Sam Bass Warner, Jr.'s term "privatism" to denote the dominant cultural tradition in the United States and Great Britain. The authors state: "It signifies an underlying confidence in the capacity of the private sector to create the conditions for personal and community prosperity. . . a belief that private institutions are intrinsically superior to public institutions for the delivery of goods and services; and a confidence that market efficiency is the appropriate criterion of social performance in virtually all spheres of community activity."[19]

Since the first Reagan administration, the term privatization has been a "political slogan to describe the movement to reduce the role of modern government and transfer back to private hands responsibilities that governments had assumed in the modern welfare state."[20] E. S. Savas, a longtime student of privatization, describes the practice as widely appealing to pragmatists, right-wing ideologues, commercial interests, and populists alike: "The goal of the pragmatists is better government, in the sense of a more cost-effective one. The goal of those who approach the matter ideologically is less government, one that plays a smaller role vis-a-vis private institutions. The goal of commercial interests is to get more business by having more of government's spending redirected toward them. And the goal of the populists is to achieve a better society by giving people greater power to satisfy their common needs, while diminishing that of large public and private bureaucracies."[21]

But the National Academy of Public Administration warns that while "privatization is supposed to reduce costs and increase efficiency by injecting a degree of market discipline into government operations . . . the presence of competition cannot simply be assumed when services are privatized. . . . Significant barriers to entry can impede competition and private providers can form 'cartels' that reduce the scope of market incentives."[22] Certainly this is a possibility with respect to resident management, where tenancy in a public housing project is required as a condition of employment. A 1986 evaluation of a resident-managed public housing project in Louisville, Kentucky, for example, attributed the inadequate level of property upkeep to the inability of the resident management company to recruit a sufficient number of qualified maintenance personnel from the tenant population.[23]

Privatization advocates assert that selling public housing to residents is more cost-effective than retaining the housing in public ownership. But there has been insufficient empirical analysis to justify this claim. According to HUD's inspector general, who reviewed the department's public housing resident management and homeownership programs in 1989, "Most of the existing evaluation data on the effectiveness of these programs is incomplete and conflicting."[24]

Since there are no empirical studies that support the efficiency claims of its advocates, there may be more than an element of truth in John D. Donahue's proposition that "to go from the observation that private companies tend to do what they do better than public agencies, to the assertion that companies should take over the agencies' duties, is rather like observing that the clients of exercise spas are healthier, on average, than the clients of hospitals, and concluding from this that workout coaches should take over for doctors. Public tasks are different, and mostly harder."[25]

Further, as economist Janet Pack noted, "any reorganization of service delivery has distributional consequences—even where the only intention is to achieve an efficiency improvement."[26] Selling off public housing units reduces the inventory and alters the composition and location of a community's low-income rental housing; it can fundamentally change the socioeconomic mix of the tenant population. Whether the consequences will be good or bad for the program, the public housing residents, or the community has not yet been determined.

Far more powerful in the privatization debate is the populists' case for privatizing public housing, based on the argument that, like many other public institutions, housing authorities have become "too institutionalized, too bureaucratized, too professionalized, too protective of their own interests," and increasingly unresponsive to the needs of the people they were created to serve.[27]

Resident management, it is claimed, can empower the poor by giving them a "sense that they now can be the ones who at least can exert some influence over what happens to them."[28] Homeownership, it is argued, would be an even more powerful liberating force by severing the chains of dependency between tenants and their landlords.

To some conservatives, public housing symbolizes the failings of New Deal emergency-relief efforts that created a "professional class of social policy bureaucrats and a corps of sociologists, psychologists and social workers who, in effect, formed a social service industry with its own social status, goals, and interests. . . ."[29] The view that public housing is part of an extensive, self-serving "poverty industry," staffed by individuals who have "a vested interest in dependency and in the client relationships of the poor," pervades the privatization literature.[30] So, too, does the belief that "solutions to the economic and social problems of minority and low-income communities in the United States will continue to elude us as long as we ignore the reality that those who are experiencing the problems have little or no voice in designing solutions to those problems."[31]

Resident management and public housing homeownership policies are also being promoted by an expanding, politically conservative segment of the black community that espouses what it refers to as "opportunity society approaches to solving the problems of the inner city poor."[32] They "repudiate the widely held notion that government solutions are intrinsically better and more effective than self-help entrepreneurial strategies that tap resources with the Black community."[33] Robert L. Woodson, head of the nonprofit National Center for Neighborhood Enterprise and an unofficial adviser to HUD Secretary Jack Kemp, writes: "Operating multimillion dollar budgets, resident managers have turned crime-ridden hell-holes into healthy communities that place a premium on education, family and self-motivation. . . . Scores of small businesses and hundreds of jobs have been created, crime, vandalism have decreased, teenage pregnancy statistics have been reversed and fathers and husbands have returned to abandoned families. At the same time, administrative costs have been drastically reduced, vacant apartments repaired, and rent collections doubled and tripled."[34]

The actual record of the fewer than twenty public housing resident management entities formed since the early 1970s, however, is decidedly mixed.

The British Model

Great Britain's decade-old right-to-buy law is the ideological forerunner of the Reagan administration privatization scheme.

The ideological basis of the British right-to-buy policy is explained by British policy analyst Stuart Butler of the Heritage Foundation: "Approximately 40 percent of British families were living in government-owned units, and such public housing constituted a considerable drain on the Treasury. . . . The conservatives recognized that they could never hope to recoup the cost of operating housing by extracting higher rents from the tenants. So they gave the tenants the right to buy their units at discounts of up to 50 percent of market value. In this way, the government eliminated costly operating subsidies on each unit sold, obtained an immediate infusion of cash, and turned dependent tenants into independent owners."[35]

As early as 1966, local councils (i.e., authorities), which owned nearly three-quarters of the British rental housing stock, were authorized to sell existing units to tenants who had been in place for at least three years. There were relatively few sales, though, because most local councils were controlled by the Labour party, which opposed privatization. This situation changed with the election of the Thatcher government in 1979. Central-government-financed council housing starts began a dramatic decline that continues to this day. Between 1976 and 1986, housing starts by local authorities in Britain dropped more than 90 percent, from 116,000 to 16,000 units. In 1980, tenants were given a statutory right to buy their units.[36] Since then, nearly one million council tenants have exercised their right to buy—generally selecting the newer, higher-quality, better-located council houses.[37]

When sales slowed, the government made the offer harder to refuse. According to Mike Elbro, head of the London-based Institute of Housing, there is now "the right to buy, the right to part purchase, and the right to require a mortgage from the local authority. The discounts now available range from 44 percent to 70 percent of market value, depending on the length of occupation, subject to a maximum discount of 50,000 pounds" (the rough equivalent of $75,000 U.S. dollars).[38]

With few new council houses being built, and with the removal from the rental supply of more than a million council houses, fewer rental opportunities are now available to the lower-income households that cannot afford to buy a home. There is some indication that this has restricted mobility and had some impact on local labor markets—especially in the south, where the economy is strong, the demand for housing is high, and local councils lost more than a third of their housing stock in the 1980s. As a result, labor availability has been reduced and the problems of homelessness have been exacerbated.

Paradoxically, even though "the typical buyer of British public housing is a skilled worker with above average wages, and often with more than one wage earner in the household,"[39] privatization of council housing in Britain has increased the level of dependency on state benefits by both homeowners and council tenants alike. Between 1979 and 1984, the number of homeowners in receipt of state benefits rose from 4 percent to 5 percent; the proportion of council tenants on benefits rose from 21 percent to 34 percent.[40]

Part of the reason for this is that, despite the deep discounts, most buyers of council housing substantially increased their monthly housing costs—up to 100 percent or more in some areas.[41] According to Elbro, "The recent series of mortgage rate increases in the UK, from 9.5 percent to 15 percent, have caused severe difficulties for recent entrants to the owner-occupied sector, and problems with mortgage arrears are currently rapidly growing."[42] Some critics of Britain's privatization policy worry that the government's need to bail out financially troubled homeowners will siphon subsidies away from low-income renters to moderate-income homeowners.

A more significant problem is the impact of the right-to-buy policy on the unsold council housing stock. There is growing concern that privatization has reduced the diversity of public housing stock and lowered its average quality.[43] British housing advocates fear that local councils are becoming the housers of last resort— much as their American public housing authority counterparts— now that they are "disproportionately housing the unemployed, the families on state incomes, and the elderly. . . . 'Welfare housing,' seen at its most extreme in American cities, is excessively socially divisive, often dangerously insecure, expensive to manage and maintain, badly appointed and often badly constructed and ill served by commercial, social, educational, transport, medical and employment facilities. . . . Few people live there from choice."[44]

With Britain's homeownership rate approaching 70 percent and council housing sales now down to a trickle, the emphasis of the Thatcher government's housing policy shifted back to the rental sector. The 1988 Housing Act was an attempt to reinvigorate the private rental sector, which currently holds just 21 percent of the total rental stock, by deregulating private rents, restructuring the finances of nonprofit housing associations, and offering public-sector tenants the opportunity to change landlords.[45] According to a November 1988 Department of the Environment news release: "For the first time councils will have to compete with alternative landlords, and this will mean treating their tenants as consumers instead of—as some do—as dependents."[46]

In short, the prevailing sentiment among British housing policy-makers continues to be that local councils are ineffective, overly bureaucratic, and insensitive housing managers that will have to shape up or lose their constituency in a more competitive market environment. Why private landlords or housing associations with little financial help from the government should be able to successfully reverse the fortunes of council estates is not immediately apparent. Nor, for that matter, is the reason why British housing policies have become a model for privatizing public housing in the United States.

A final criticism of the British right-to-buy policy that could be relevant to the United States has to do with the reduction of budgets for low-income housing. One of the arguments favoring the sale of council housing in Britain was that the proceeds could be used to supplement shrinking government allocations for new production and renovations. According to Butler, however, this argument "has been progressively discredited by a series of decisions to restrict the proportion of [sales] receipts Local Authorities can use for this purpose."[47]

Critics of the Bush administration's housing policies view privatization as a harbinger of a continued federal retreat from assisted housing. But the fact that a large-scale effort to sell public housing could end up costing the government more, not less, was recognized by HUD as early as 1984: "A substantial program of sales of public housing to tenants would decrease the number of units available in the public housing rental program, and could ultimately lead to the pressure from Congress to build new units to replace those lost. . . . Inevitably, debt obligation assumed by the federal government for new units will be substantially higher than that on the units sold, because of increases in the cost of developing public housing over time."[48]

In an October 1989 assessment of privatization activities, HUD's inspector general recognized the constraint that one-for-one replacement would have on public housing sales and recommended a change in federal law to break the link between sales and new production.[49]

In its first year in office, the Bush administration proposed legislation to eliminate the one-for-one replacement provision associated with project buy-outs, while HUD's fiscal 1991 budget contains funds for ten-year housing vouchers (to help displaced families pay private-sector rents) as an alternative to more public housing construction. Clearly, the future of privatization in the United States hinges on the resolution of the replacement-housing issue.

Chapter 3

LOW-INCOME HOMEOWNERSHIP PROGRAMS AND PUBLIC HOUSING

Homeownership is in decline in the United States. This national trend is especially evident in the percentage of twenty-five- to twenty-nine-year-olds who own their own homes—their number dropped from 44 percent in 1979 to 36.2 percent in 1987.

To help reverse this trend, several members of Congress have introduced bills to make financing a home easier. Senators Alan Cranston and Alfonse D'Amato introduced a bill that would extend the authority of states and localities to administer tax-exempt revenue bond and mortgage-credit certificate programs. Their bill as well as the Bush administration's Homeownership Opportunities for People Everywhere (HOPE) initiative would permit first-time homebuyers to withdraw funds for a down payment from either their IRA or other tax-sheltered retirement accounts without a tax penalty. The Cranston–D'Amato bill would also reduce down payment requirements to as little as 3 percent on FHA-insured mortgages. To reduce the burden of high mortgage interest rates, House Banking Committee Chairman Henry Gonzalez proposed creating a national housing trust fund that would subsidize mortgage interest rates down to 6 percent for first-time homebuyers. The subsidy would become a lien on the house, repayable without interest on the sale of the property. But these efforts are targeted to the middle class; very little is being done to help poor families to become homeowners.

While the federal government has long maintained a mix of low-income rental and homeownership programs, new allocations for low-income homeownership programs continue to be reduced. According to the Congressional Budget Office, the "proportion of all assisted households that receive[d] homeownership assistance . . . declined from 34 percent at the beginning of 1977 to less than 20 percent at the beginning of 1988 [and] the number of commitments . . . being processed (26,600) is less than the number of households expected to leave the program in 1988, resulting in a net decline in the number of homeowners served."[1] Out of a total of 5.5 million households currently receiving federal housing assistance, only about 1.2 million are homeowners.

The Rationale for More Homeownership Programs

One argument for increasing low-income homeownership assistance is that for years the poor have not been getting their fair share of federal housing subsidies. To give one example, the amount of money spent on all low-income subsidized housing programs during the 1980s ($107.7 billion) is approximately equal to the amount of federal tax expenditures for all homeowners in just the past two years ($107.4 billion).[2] President Bush's budget estimates that these same tax breaks for homeowners will exceed $80 billion in fiscal 1991 alone. This tax break is more then five times greater than all HUD budget outlays for assisted housing and forty times bigger than the administration's new HOPE homeownership initiative.[3]

These tax benefits to homeowners are rarely viewed as subsidies—in direct contrast to low-income housing assistance. J. Kemeny, a British housing policy analyst, states that "tax deductibility and exemptions, as well as the various other forms of indirect subsidy . . . do not carry the stigma associated with the payments of subsidies to 'public' housing . . . therefore readily permit[ting] homeowners to be defined as 'paying their way' in housing, as against those who are unable to do so and must be 'supported by the state.'"[4]

Further, these federal tax expenditures for homeowners favor the most affluent: According to the Low Income Housing Information Service, of the $50.6 billion total housing tax expenditures in 1988, "$33.6 billion, or 66.4 percent of the benefits went to households with incomes of $50,000 or more. When low-income housing outlays and housing tax expenditures are combined, households with incomes of $50,000 or more received . . . 52.2 percent of the total."[5]

Another argument for low-income homeownership programs is that, to the extent that home equity is an asset and constitutes wealth, homeownership assistance would remedy current inequalities in the opportunity to accumulate wealth.

Joint Center for Housing Studies researchers at Harvard University state that, in 1988, equity in a house accounted for more than 54 percent of the average homeowner's net wealth ($44,535/$83,010). Though both net wealth and home equity were lower among black owners, home equity accounted for fully 80 percent of their net wealth ($29,284/$36,589). Among Hispanics, home equity represented virtually all of the household's wealth—98 percent ($67,458/$69,137).

Because equity in a house represents a very large portion of a household's net wealth, homeownership assistance could be especially important to low-income minorities.

For a variety of reasons (including racial discrimination), home-ownership rates are substantially lower among minorities—poor and nonpoor alike—than they are for whites. According to the Joint Center for Housing Studies, "In 1985 some 40 percent of all Hispanic house-holds, 44 percent of all black households, and 68 percent of all white households were homeowners. In fact, the proportion of poor white households that own their homes—46 percent—is greater than either the proportion of all black or all Hispanic households that are homeowners."[6]

William C. Apgar argues that "the lack of homeownership oppor-tunities for blacks has undermined their ability to accumulate wealth." It is reasonable, therefore, to conclude that properly structured sales programs could help remedy this injustice.[7]

The majority of public housing residents are low-income minority, as are more than 90 percent of all homebuyers in HUD's national Public Housing Homeownership Demonstration, which provides public housing residents an opportunity to buy their apartments at substantial discounts. Even with this homeownership assistance, however, resale restrictions and market limitations will affect the extent of equity buildup for these homebuyers, as market application rates in predominately minority neighborhoods tend to lag behind those in white areas.[8]

There is another argument in favor of low-income homeownership programs: If the program is targeted to higher-income, more upwardly mobile occupants of assisted rental housing developments, their departure would free up these units for poorer families on the wait-ing list. This means that the federal government could expand its over-all assisted-housing program at lower cost than if it just continued building more public housing.

Although there has been little systematic economic analysis of this idea, it is likely that the cost to the government of subsidizing a higher-end assisted renter to become a homeowner would be less than adding one new unit to the low-income rental stock. According to HUD, it costs around $69,000 to build a new public housing unit. (This cost would, of course, be much higher in major urban areas like New York City, Boston, and San Francisco.) The operating subsidy required to keep the rent affordable to the very poor over the economic life of the unit would add another $10,000 to $15,000 (in present value terms) to the cost. If a federal homeownership program could free up an existing low-income unit by helping a renting family become a homeowning family at a long-term cost of less than $79,000 a unit, then it would be more cost-effective than building new public housing.

The marginal cost to the federal government of keeping a low-income family in an ownership situation is also lower than the cost of continuing rental assistance. In fiscal 1987, for example, the federal outlay per household assisted under HUD's Section 235 and Farmers Home Administration's Section 502 homeownership assistance programs averaged just $1,906—considerably lower than the average direct federal outlay for a recipient of a Section 8 rental certificate or housing voucher, which was $3,013.

President Bush's HOPE initiative is promising in this regard. It calls for the use of Section 8 certificates and vouchers to subsidize homeownership costs, and would convert certificate and voucher long-term budget authority into a front-end capital grant to help low-income tenants buy and convert privately owned rental projects into limited equity co-ops.

Many public housing directors would argue, however, that the issue at hand is not simply whether it is cheaper to subsidize a family to move out of public housing than to build a new public housing rental unit. Rather, they claim, the real issue is whether privatizing public housing further segregates very poor and dependent populations in government-owned complexes.

Federal Low-Income Homeownership Programs

Section 235. In 1968, HUD's largest low-income homeownership initiative was enacted into law: the Section 235 interest-subsidy program. Between 1969 and 1979, Section 235 generated subsidized mortgages for some 529,000 low-income homebuyers. (The bulk of program activity occurred between 1969 and 1973.) But its success was tempered: the subsidy formula made it difficult for some homebuyers to keep up with inflationary increases in costs; one out of five homebuyers lost their homes; and the administration of the program was plagued by an extraordinary degree of mismanagement and corruption.

The federal government never systematically evaluated the Section 235 program. But government audits and congressional studies of scandals connected to the program provide some insights on what went wrong.

In 1968, when Section 235 was enacted, the goal of a decent home in a good environment for every American family still seemed far out of reach. In an attempt to accelerate progress toward that goal, Congress legislated the construction and rehabilitation of twenty-six million housing units—of which six million would be targeted to low- and moderate-income families—within a ten-year time frame.

Section 235 of the Housing Act of 1968 established a mortgage-interest-subsidy program for families with incomes below 135 percent of public housing income limits. Depending on a household's income, the federal government would subsidize home-ownership costs all the way down to the equivalent of a 1 percent mortgage. The Section 235 subsidy was for "the lesser of either (1) the differences between (a) 20 percent of monthly adjusted income and (b) the total monthly payment under the mortgage for principal, interest, mortgage insurance premium, taxes and hazard insurance; or (2) the difference between (a) the monthly payment for principal, interest and the mortgage insurance premium, and (b) the payment to principal and interest at a 1 percent interest rate."[9]

The minimum down payment was set at $200, and the long-standing rule that all FHA-insured loans must meet an "economic soundness" test was replaced by a less stringent test that merely required both buyers and houses to be "reasonable risks." According to Brian Boyer, "In practice, this meant that less rigorous criteria for housing conditions were accepted, as long as the requirements of all state laws, or local ordinances or regulations relating to the public health or safety zoning . . . were met."[10]

Subsidy payments would be made either throughout the term of the mortgage, until the property was sold, or until the homeowner could pay the full monthly mortgage payment at the unsubsidized rate (including interest, insurance, and taxes) from 20 percent of income.[11]

But fixing the maximum amount of assistance at the difference between a market rate and a 1 percent mortgage gave higher subsidies to higher-income families who bought more expensive houses. It also placed an extra financial burden on the poorest program participants because, once the maximum subsidy level was reached, all increases in taxes and insurance had to be paid out of the home-buyer's own pocket. The fact that subsidies are based on adjusted incomes—allowing deductions for each dependent minor—also gave higher subsidies to higher-income buyers, who tend to have larger families than lower-income buyers.[12]

In its first three years of operation, from 1969 to 1972, nearly 400,000 low- and moderate-income families received Section 235 mortgage loans—accounting for nearly 10 percent of all single-family housing starts during this period and a much higher percentage of lower-priced construction.[13] This unprecedented level of assistance was part of a larger government effort to promote homeownership opportunities in an attempt to calm the crisis atmosphere gripping so many American cities.

Phil Brownstein, a former FHA commissioner, described the turmoil and the rationale behind this effort: "Not only was this country involved in a war in Vietnam, but it was also facing internal crisis at home. . . . The opportunity of homeownership for the poor was thought to be an appropriate response to the fear and unrest resulting from the riots and near-riots in many of our metropolitan areas. For those willing and able to accept the responsibility, homeownership was deemed a worthy aspiration, one which would afford qualified purchasers the hope and opportunity of entering the mainstream of American life."[14]

According to HUD, in 1970 alone, "about 470,000 subsidized units—more than twice as many as in any previous year—were started or substantially rehabilitated under all HUD and Farmers Home Administration programs. The new subsidized starts amounted to almost 30 percent of all housing starts in 1970; and the numbers were similar in 1971."[15]

Further, the number of families participating in the program that were able to improve their financial situation to the point where they no longer needed further subsidies was high. According to Brownstein, at the end of fiscal 1976, fully 37 percent of all Section 235 homebuyers had no further need for the subsidy.[16] The Library of Congress estimates that this success rate had grown to approximately half of all families by 1980.[17]

Unfortunately, though, HUD's management of this extraordinary assisted-housing effort was terribly lax and plagued by scandals. There was no single cause of the scandals. Certainly, the elimination of the economic-soundness requirement in mortgage underwriting contributed. So did the tremendously increased workload for unsophisticated FHA employees (one investigator claimed "the FHA staff knew about as much about the inner city housing market and ghetto business practices as Pope Paul knows about the Mob") reported to have a "public-be-damned" attitude.[18]

According to Brian Boyer, an investigative reporter for the *Detroit Free Press*, who won a Pulitzer Prize for his coverage of Section 235 scandals, "The scandal was officially touched off January 6, 1971, when the House Committee on Banking and Currency issued a report that detailed 102 specific cases of FHA crimes. Doubting that it was so, HUD sent out its Office of Investigation to double check on the allegations. The investigators interviewed 511 individuals in thirty days. They found forty-one prima facie cases of Federal fraud against the FHA and forty-five additional cases of false statements and certifications concerning required repairs, mortgagor investments, and ownership of properties, forged certifications and fraudulent appraisal reports."[19]

By the time the dust settled, it was determined that 26 percent of all Section 235 loans for new houses and 43 percent of the loans on used houses were made for either substandard or uninhabitable properties.[20]

In 1975, an article in *Barron's* magazine described a typical Section 235 transaction as follows: "A developer would purchase several homes in poor condition on which cosmetic repairs would be made. An inflated estimate of the property value would then be obtained from HUD, at which time the house would be sold to an unsuspecting, unsophisticated purchaser. Shortly after the homeowner moved in, it became evident the house had major faults making it virtually unlivable. This sets off a chain reaction: first, as the homeowner has no money to make repairs, the house deteriorates further. Eventually, as a result of the substandard conditions, the homeowner decides to abandon the home; the lender than [sic] transfers the vacant home to HUD. Concurrently, the home is vandalized, and remains vacant in its blighted condition for numerous months while remaining in the HUD inventory. Meanwhile, other homes on the block begin to undergo a similar process, whereby a snowballing effort takes hold and other homes are abandoned and transferred to HUD, and the vicious cycle continues."[21]

The combination of sloppy and fraudulent underwriting, the failure to properly counsel potential homebuyers about the responsibilities of homeownership, a subsidy formula that put a financial squeeze on the lowest-income buyers, as well as mismanagement and fraud, understandably led to high failure rates. As of year-end 1979, out of a total of 528,885 mortgages assisted under the program, slightly more than 108,000—one in five—had been either foreclosed upon or, in lieu of foreclosure, assigned to FHA.[22]

Considering the extent of mismanagement and outright fraud that took place in the administration of Section 235, such a high failure rate is not surprising; given the high-risk nature of the program, the failure rate does not even seem so bad. The real question—raised by Brownstein, who played a major role in designing the program—was how to increase the success rate of high-risk social programs.[23] It is a question that remains relevant today.

HUD's Turnkey III Program. Though little known, the public housing program had its first homeownership component in 1968: the Turnkey III Homeownership Opportunities Program.[24] The Turnkey III program was funded by Congress for just five years, from 1969 to 1973. Under this program, public housing authorities were authorized to develop projects for eventual sale to lower-income families. It worked as follows: "A tenant homebuyer takes occupancy under a lease-purchase agreement, which provides for an initial period of tenancy with opportunity to build up equity credits toward purchase after some period of years."[25]

The program produced 263 projects and a total of 6,010 dwelling units. Only 2,932 homes (less than 18 percent) produced under the program have been sold; the vast majority remain under management by public housing authorities as part of their conventional public housing rental inventories.[26]

Although no comprehensive evaluation of Turnkey III has been carried out, an informal survey by HUD indicates that the "units do not have the traditional public housing project stigma because they are usually scattered sites, and not particularly known to neighborhoods as public housing. This housing is usually the best looking, better maintained public housing in the community."[27] Also on the positive side, there is generally a low vacancy and turnover rate in Turnkey III projects; homebuyers have generally fulfilled their responsibility for routine maintenance of the units; and, in many instances, considerable improvements have been made to these units.

Still, the program has suffered major problems. Homebuyers' families generally receive insufficient orientation and ongoing counseling. High interest rates have made it difficult for low-income families to get mortgages. Homebuyers and homeowners associations have shown little or no interest in the program. And, in many instances, in order to attract participants, income limits had to be waived.

Most of these findings were confirmed in a formal review of the Turnkey III program carried out by the HUD inspector general in 1984. The review covered 4,277 units, of which only 8 percent had been sold. According to the report: "The PHAs did not diligently pursue sales of Program Units. Specifically, the public housing authorities did not: require financially able tenants to purchase their units; evict under-income tenants; and properly screen tenants for homeownership potential."[28]

Section 502. The Farmers Home Administration administers a variety of housing programs for residents of rural areas, the largest and most successful of which is the Section 502 homeownership program authorized in 1949. Operating in a manner similar to HUD's Section 235 program, Section 502 has provided nearly a million families with mortgage loans.

Under Section 502, the Farmers Home Administration provides long-term loans with no down payment. The subsidy is in the form of an interest credit that reduces the borrower's interest rate to as low as 1 percent. (As in HUD's Section 235 program, the interest paid by the borrower rises and falls with household income.)[29] The borrower must pay at least 20 percent of income for mortgage principal, interest, taxes, and property insurance—or the same costs based on a 1 percent mortgage, whichever is higher.[30]

A recent assessment of the Section 502 program was conducted by the Housing Assistance Council. A sample of 894 rural households that obtained Section 502 loans in 1981 was chosen and tracked for five years.

The sampling broke down as follows: A quarter of the borrowers were minority. The average age was thirty-two years; 7 percent were over the age of fifty-five. Three-fifths of the households were headed by married couples; two-fifths by a single person (usually female). Ninety percent were employed, mostly in low-wage or seasonal industries, or self-employed. The median income was just $9,750; 28 percent had incomes below the 1981 poverty threshold.[31] About a quarter of the sample had income from nonemployment sources including AFDC, Social Security, disability, pensions, and child support. Ten percent relied solely on these sources of income; 3 percent depended on AFDC alone.[32]

The Housing Assistance Council assessment showed that, as of 1986, most borrowers were actually ahead in their mortgage payments. Another 20 percent were current. Still, 7.3 percent had lost their homes because they were not able to keep up with their loan obligations, while another 23 percent were behind in their mortgage payments. Of the latter, 7 percent were seriously delinquent, behind in their payments by three months or more. Despite these losses, the overall review was a good one.

The average annual subsidy had declined from $3,300 to $2,484. About 13 percent of all borrowers were able to eliminate the interest credit entirely, despite the fact that over half—53 percent—of all program participants had started with the maximum subsidy. Even though borrowers receiving the maximum subsidy frequently relied on Social Security or AFDC payments as their primary source of income, as a group these very-low-income homebuyers had shown excellent repayment performance.

Some Lessons Learned

Local Administration. Farmers Home Administration programs, which are administered at the county level, were much more successful than the more centralized HUD programs, which operate through a network of area offices whose jurisdictions can cover one or more states. According to the Housing Assistance Council, the "personal servicing" provided by Farmers Home Administration county offices "has been important in preventing and resolving delinquencies."[33] In contrast, a Library of Congress study of HUD's Section 235 program indicated that "extreme decentralization of program administration [from HUD central to area offices] was followed by substantial laxity and corruption in property and credit underwriting."[34] The scandals aside, the combination of a government policy that relaxed underwriting standards in riot-torn inner cities, coupled with the fact that mortgage approvals and loan servicing were frequently accomplished a hundred miles or more from where the loan originated, contributed to the program's troubles. Clearly, the lesson is that low-income homeownership programs should be locally administered and serviced.

The Importance of Counseling. The second lesson is that pre- and postpurchase counseling must be integral components of low-income homeownership programs. This is especially important when little or no down payment or other up-front commitment (such as sweat equity, or self-help labor) is required from the homebuyer.

The importance of counseling was underscored in the Housing Assistance Council study referred to above, which suggested that when counseling was available in Farmers Home Administration county offices, "borrowers have often been able to improve their ability to manage their household finances."[35] Brownstein concurs that "it is simply not enough to provide individuals with keys to a house, mortgage payment book, and then walk away. . . . an uncounseled homeowner is easy prey for salesmen selling everything from fire alarms to picket fences, especially when the cost is described in terms of pennies a day."[36]

The most systematic assessment of housing counseling was conducted for HUD in 1983.[37] Among the findings was the fact that those most likely to benefit from housing counseling are unlikely to volunteer for help. Thus, housing counseling should be made a mandatory component of low-income homeownership programs. The study also made clear that an important function of prepurchase counseling is to identify and prevent families who do not have the temperament or the financial or family resources from entering homeownership programs.

The study found that more foreclosures were due to illness and employment problems than to poor money management. Counseling, of course, cannot resolve these short-run financial emergencies; homeownership programs must have well-capitalized operating and replacement reserves to deal with them. But in those instances where poor money management is the cause of the homebuyers' problems, postpurchase counseling assistance could make a significant difference.

But the study's most frequently cited finding is that housing counseling is not cost-effective. In defining cost-effectiveness, though, the researchers placed equal weight on a federal dollar spent on counseling to keep a family in its home and a dollar spent to pay off a bank on a foreclosed mortgage. Also, since, for HUD, the "costs of acquiring, repairing, maintaining, and eventually selling the property were about equal to the cost of continued subsidies to homeowners whose foreclosures were avoided" through counseling, the researchers concluded that housing counseling was not particularly cost-effective.[38] Relying solely on such economic analysis, without taking into account the human and societal perspective, does not make good housing policy. Nonetheless, this finding, unfortunately, has discouraged federal funding of housing counseling programs.

Still, cities across the country are including mandatory counseling in their low-income homeownership programs. One example is in Jefferson County (Louisville), Kentucky. The Jefferson County Homeownership Program counsels families on how to establish a good credit history as well as on budgeting and savings, so that they can meet down payment and closing costs on a home. The success of this local program is reflected in the statement made by one participant that "[when] my husband, David, and I entered the program . . . we were heavily in debt and didn't know which way to turn. . . . Naturally, we were pleased with the prospect of owning our own home, but more importantly, we would learn lifetime lessons in handling our finances. . . . We now have a budget that we follow, we pay our bills on time, and have our priorities straight. We have paid off all but two of our bills in just five months. . . . If everything continues to go well, we will be able to . . . buy a home in 1990. . . . Our lives have been turned around and we can look forward to the future."[39]

Long-term Affordability. Another lesson is that counseling can carry a financially troubled homeowner just so far. Experience with low-income homeownership programs has shown that unanticipated increases in such costs as property taxes and insurance, utilities and upkeep, can play havoc with low-income homebuyers' inelastic budgets.[40] The Housing Assistance Council five-year assessment of the Farmers Home Administration Section 502 program found, for example, that for a tenth of all borrowers, property taxes and insurance increased by more than $1,000 a year.[41]

Long-term affordability also has been questioned by HUD's Office of Policy Development and Research, which noted that the problem of initial affordability is compounded by "the disparity between the increase in income of lower-income families and the increase in operating costs over time."[42] The Farmers Home Administration noted that "the cost of operating a single-family home in the past decade rose at an annual rate of 11.5 percent per year. Data from the Annual Housing Survey indicates that tenant incomes grew at a 7.7 percent yearly rate between 1974 and 1980. Thus, the difference between what a tenant could afford and the cost of operating a home could be expected to grow over time, creating even more problems of affordability for lower-income families."[43]

The early evidence on homeowner delinquency and default in HUD's Public Housing Homeownership Demonstration is that failure rates probably will be in the neighborhood of 10 percent. As of the end of August 1989, five of the demonstration's twelve active sales programs had already experienced a problem with late payments or more serious borrower delinquencies. Within the first eighteen months of closing on their homes, about 31 percent of all buyers indicated that their mortgage payments were causing a strain on their budgets, and 10 percent said they were already in arrears on their payments by at least one month.[44]

Low-income families who take advantage of federal homeownership programs are not exclusively public housing tenants. But the new privatization efforts are focused on that population and are heavily influenced by such features of public housing programs as continuing operating subsidies. What follows is an overview of public housing in the United States—who it serves, how it is financed, and how it is managed.

An Overview of the Public Housing Program[45]

Public housing, it has been said, is unpopular with everybody except the people who live in it and the people who are waiting to get in. This is not an insignificant population. More than 1.3 million families currently occupy public housing units, and nearly 800,000 more are on the waiting list.

Public housing accounts for about 5 percent of all rental housing in the nation, and for as much as 15 percent of rental housing (and a much higher percentage of low-rent stock) in many central cities—that is, in metropolitan areas with over 50,000 in population. Further, the demand for more public housing is high—and increasing. In a survey conducted for the U.S. Conference of Mayors in 1987, the demand for low-income housing increased by an average of 40 percent in 88 percent of the cities considered. With just 17,000 vacant public housing units available for rent nationwide at any one time, the demand, in 1987, outstripped supply by a ratio of 46:1.

HUD argues that such vacancy figures understate capacity and suggests that a better measure is the number of public housing units that become available each year due to turnover—currently averaging 14 percent nationally, or almost 200,000 public housing opportunities.

Nonetheless, the wait for public housing is long. The average wait for public housing nationwide is about thirteen months. For 9 percent of all public housing authorities, the average wait exceeds three years. In many cities it is much longer than that: seven years in Atlantic City, New Jersey; five years in Winston-Salem, North Carolina; and ten years in Jersey City, New Jersey.

Perception versus Reality. Because a sizable share of the nation's poor—especially single-parent minority poor—live in public housing, its image is overwhelmingly negative. The common perception is that most public housing projects consist of large, ugly developments that are poorly maintained and managed; that they contain concentrations of large, minority families with undisciplined children and high crime rates; and that they have a negative impact on the surrounding community.

In fact, though, just 27 percent of all public housing developments are high-rise buildings; 32 percent are garden apartments; 16 percent are low-rise, walk-up apartments; and 25 percent are single-family or townhouse structures. Although high-rise projects—three-quarters of which are in the largest cities—represent a relatively small portion of the public housing stock, the terrible living environments they create led Congress, in 1968, to prohibit further construction of this type of public housing for families with children (unless there is no practical alternative).[46] Today, such high-rise public housing construction is reserved for projects built expressly for the elderly—to the extent that there is any new public housing development at all.

Who Lives in Public Housing. Contrary to common perception, the majority of public housing residents are not welfare-dependent single women with children. About 38 percent are elderly, and, according to the Council of Large Public Housing Authorities, a "small but growing percentage of public housing is occupied by young and middle-aged single people with some sort of handicap, many of whom would be homeless otherwise."[47] While single-parent households account for a significant proportion of public housing residents, a large segment of the population is composed of married couples without children. There also are some traditional two-parent families as well. Further, despite high rates of welfare dependency among single-parent families, about 42 percent of all nonelderly households in public housing include a wage earner.

The families and individuals who live in public housing are generally very poor—and have been growing poorer. Between 1950 and 1970, for example, the median income of public housing tenants fell from 64 percent to 37 percent of the national median. Between 1974 and 1981, the number of tenants with incomes between 10 percent and 30 percent of the national median rose from 60 percent to 65 percent.

In 1988, public housing tenants had an average income of only $6,539 compared to $32,144 for all American households. Thus, the typical public housing family had less than 25 percent of the national average income.[48] Contrary to popular opinion, incomes of blacks and whites in public housing are not significantly different.

Most public housing tenants are racial and ethnic minorities: 38 percent are white, 49 percent are black, and 13 percent are Hispanic and members of other minority groups. But in large urban areas, 83 percent of public housing households are minority.

Managing Public Housing. Public housing authorities are dispersed throughout the nation, but they are most heavily concentrated in the southeast (26 percent) and southwest (27 percent). The average public housing authority manages just 403 units (87 percent manage fewer than 500 units; 8 percent manage between 501 and 1,250 units; and the remaining 5 percent manage more than 1,250 units). The 140 public housing authorities in the last category manage 60 percent of the nation's public housing stock; the 15 largest public housing authorities in this group manage 30 percent of the stock. New York

City, with 173,000 public housing units, is the largest of the nation's public housing authorities.

With the enormous diversity—large- and small-scale programs; new and old programs; programs in big cities, suburban communities, and rural areas; and programs managing buildings that range from densely built high-rises to scattered-site, single-family and townhouse-type dwellings—one of the greatest challenges facing HUD and Congress is promulgating rules, regulations, and laws relating to public housing that can be consistently applied.

Operating Subsidies and Regulations. The United States Housing Act of 1937, which created the public housing program, restricted the federal contribution to paying for bricks and mortar; tenant rents had to cover the full costs of operation. According to Wayne Sherwood and Elizabeth March of the Council of Large Public Housing Authorities, "The system functioned relatively well for about 25 years—a period during which the building stock remained in good condition and the tenant population was composed largely of the working poor."[49]

By the mid-1960s, though, the system was in trouble. This was due, in large measure, to radically changing conditions:

> The 1949 Housing Act, which prohibited discrimination against welfare recipients and gave priority to those displaced by the Urban Renewal Program, as well as the post-war move to the North by many Southern blacks and the move into FHA-insured housing by working families, brought an increasing number of very-low-income families into public housing. With a growing proportion of tenants on low, fixed incomes, an increasing need for social services and the rising cost of maintaining an aging building stock, the rental receipts of PHAs were no longer sufficient to cover the cost of operation. Many housing authorities were forced to raise rents to levels which required tenants to pay a high proportion of their income for shelter, in some cases as much as 80 percent.[50]

In 1961, to help deal with these problems, Congress authorized a $10 monthly special subsidy for each elderly family being housed. With the exception of this $10 subsidy, though, public housing authorities still had to meet virtually all their operating expenses out of rent receipts, which was becoming increasingly difficult to do.

Legislation was introduced in Congress to allow housing authorities to increase their revenues by raising the maximum income limits for continued occupancy (which would have permitted more working families to stay in public housing), but the idea wasn't adopted. Instead, in 1964, the inadequate $10 monthly subsidy was extended to all families displaced by government action (such as slum clearance, urban renewal, or highway construction).

In addition, to be eligible for this new subsidy, public housing authorities first had to have used up most of their operating reserves. Thus, efficiently managed housing authorities that had accrued reserves were penalized, while less efficient housing authorities received financial help. This was not the first time, nor would it be the last, that laws or regulations rewarded poor management.

The Housing Act of 1968 extended the $10 subsidy to two additional groups: unusually low-income and unusually large families. Despite this help, the gap between total income and total operating costs continued to grow.

Not only were these special subsidies insufficient to cover public housing authority expenses, but a second reform, enacted in 1968, reduced public housing authority rental income. It was a HUD-promulgated regulation—the "Tenant Selection and Assignment Policy"—that required servicing families for public housing on a "first come, first served" basis, thus severely reducing the public housing authorities' ability to screen applicants in terms of their ability to pay their rent.

A year later, the Housing Act of 1969, which gave rise to HUD's public housing operating subsidy system, was passed. The act contained the first so-called Brooke Amendment, which protected very-low-income tenants by capping rents at 25 percent of income. This, in effect, eliminated minimum rents in public housing and thereby substantially reduced public housing authority rental income.

To compensate public housing authorities for this lost revenue, an operating subsidy was authorized. The average operating subsidy is now roughly $145 a month for each public housing unit in the country. The subsidy must be paid for as long as the housing remains publicly owned. In fiscal 1992, the cost to the federal government will be $2.5 billion; this is $275 million more than that in fiscal 1991.

The only way the federal government can reduce the amount it spends on operating subsidies is to decrease the size of the public housing inventory. Privatizing public housing is one way to do this.

Modernizing Public Housing. The funding formula for public housing never provided for a capital-replacement reserve. But the need became clear soon enough. With one-third of all public housing buildings now more than twenty-five years old, it is a need that cannot be ignored.

In 1968, HUD responded to the need for capital-improvement funds by creating the first public housing modernization program. While it was a step in the right direction, its focus was limited. From 1968 to 1978, "modernization funds were provided by HUD, based on priorities established annually in Washington. In some years the priority would be roofs, in others, heating facilities, and in still others, energy conservation."[51] Though tremendously helpful to housing authorities with no other funds to renew their inventories, the way the program was structured made it difficult to rehabilitate an entire project. On top of that, this piecemeal approach to modernization was not cost-effective.

In 1980, Congress created the Comprehensive Improvement Assistance Program to finance modernization of older projects through loans provided to public housing authorities by HUD. To obtain funding, public housing authorities must submit comprehensive plans for upgrading whole projects and for improving their management. When the modernization is completed, the loans are forgiven.

The cost of this program has risen substantially over time. Since 1975, aggregate funding has totaled more than $12 billion (ranging from a low of $707.4 million in 1986 to a high of $2.6 billion in 1983). The Bush–Kemp fiscal 1991 budget allows for $1.85 billion in funding—nearly $80 million less than in fiscal 1990.

A 1987 study of the public housing stock indicates that, despite considerable federal investment, there is still much repair and modernization required. Abt Associates, the independent contractor retained by HUD to prepare national estimates, reported a backlog of needed repairs and improvements that would cost $21.5 billion. According to Abt, at least $9.5 billion is required to repair or replace existing structural, mechanical, and electrical systems; another $9.5 billion is needed to upgrade or change features to meet HUD standards or to enhance long-term viability. An additional $2.5 billion is necessary to finance cost-effective energy improvements, to make more public housing units accessible to the handicapped, and to deal with health threats posed by, for example, the presence of lead-based paint in older projects.

While not disputing these cost estimates, HUD has taken the position that existing standards do not require as much change as suggested by the Abt study, and that just $10.7 billion is needed to clear up the backlogged repairs and to meet federal regulations. Whether HUD or Abt is correct—or if the truth lies somewhere in between—the work that needs to be done is obviously substantial.

The financial burden on the federal government of modernizing the aging public housing stock is not likely to be reduced by privatizing public housing. Privatized or not, the stock must be modernized to be preserved. Since poor people cannot afford costly repairs, existing federal law and prudence dictate that public housing sold to low-income families must be in good physical condition before title can be transferred.

The combination of severe federal budget constraints and a solid commitment to privatization may well lead to a housing policy that disproportionately concentrates scarce resources on housing stock slated for sale, while underfinancing renovation of the rental housing inventory. Should the administration pursue this course, it would do so at the peril of accelerating the loss of tens of thousands of public housing units due to deterioration and decay.

Chapter 4
PRIVATIZING PUBLIC HOUSING

Despite all the talk about privatization, only a handful of public housing units have been sold or approved for sale by HUD. HUD's three-year (1985–88) national Public Housing Homeownership Demonstration (PHHD) made only 320 sales to tenants—just a quarter of the units HUD had hoped to sell. Sales to resident management councils—under the provisions of the 1987 Housing and Community Development Act—have not progressed past the negotiation stage.

Clearly, alternatives to these two routes to privatization must be found to meet HUD Secretary Jack Kemp and the president's goal, announced in 1990, of giving "all public housing residents in America a chance . . . to manage and control and ultimately own public housing units within three to four years."[1]

THE PUBLIC HOUSING HOMEOWNERSHIP DEMONSTRATION[2]

The Beginnings

On October 25, 1984, HUD Secretary Samuel R. Pierce announced an ambitious three-year Public Housing Homeownership Demonstration designed to enable public housing tenants to become home-owners through the purchase of their own or another public housing unit. Under the PHHD, seventeen public housing authorities agreed to sell 1,315 units of public housing over the thirty-six-month course of the demonstration.

HUD allowed the participating public housing authorities considerable leeway in establishing their own programs. Public housing authorities could select the units that they thought would be most appropriate for sale to tenants and set the prices and terms of those sales—testing a range of methods that included fee simple (outright sale), condominium, and cooperative forms of ownership.

To reduce the price of the units, HUD agreed to continue to pay the debt service on outstanding federal bonds used to finance construction and/or modernization. But the amortization of rehabilitation costs, along with all operating costs (including property taxes where applicable, maintenance, insurance, and reserves accounts—contributed from rents each month—for replacement of such things as heating and other building systems as they wear out), would be the responsibility of buyers. Public housing authorities were strongly encouraged to seek outside financing for their buyers—such as loans from private lenders, public-spirited corporations, and state housing finance agencies—rather than to attempt to finance the sales themselves.

While HUD specified four general conditions that public housing authorities had to meet in designing their programs, it left it up to the public housing authorities themselves to decide exactly how to fulfill these guidelines:

1. All properties transferred to tenants must be in good condition prior to sale.

2. A tenant who does not want to, or is financially unable to, participate in PHHD cannot be displaced involuntarily.

3. Both pre- and post-purchase counseling and training must be provided to homebuyers.

4. The program must include some means to guard against windfall profits for a minimum of five years.

In response to these general guidelines, the seventeen public housing authorities developed programs that differed widely.

What the public housing authorities had in common was a belief in the value of homeownership, the positive qualities it cultivates—self-esteem, independence, responsibility—and the possibility of upward mobility that it brings. Experienced housing authority staff understood how difficult and time-consuming it would be to prepare families for homeownership and to qualify them for mortgages, but their commitment to achieving their sales goals was strong. The leadership of dedicated program administrators, who devoted far more time and effort to the cause than could be justified by program size or budget, made the difference between success and failure.

HUD also urged public housing authorities to consider imposing permanent resale restrictions on the former public housing units to assure their continued availability to low-income homebuyers over time, but did not make such restrictions a program requirement.

Why Sell Public Housing?

One of the most misunderstood areas of privatization has to do with the motives of the sponsoring public housing authority. "Why," it is frequently asked, "should a public housing authority voluntarily choose to sell off some or all of its stock when HUD will not replace the sold units and there is such a serious shortage of low-income housing?"

In addition to a firm belief in the benefits that homeownership offers individuals, public housing authorities have identified two quite different reasons for privatizing a portion of their stock. The first is to get rid of single-family properties that are widely scattered throughout the community and therefore costly to maintain and manage. The second is to include homeownership as one feature of a comprehensive strategy to revitalize seriously deteriorated multifamily projects and the neighborhoods in which they are located.

HUD data, on the other hand, do not support these rationales. For one thing, HUD disputes public housing authorities' perceptions of the costliness of operating scattered-site housing. For another, HUD found that poor execution has offset the potentially stabilizing effects of converting multifamily rental projects to homeownership.

Shed Costly Properties. Several housing authorities perceived PHHD as an opportunity to do good for themselves while they helped their tenants. Six out of the seventeen participating public housing authorities chose to sell some or all of their scattered-site single-family inventories on the grounds that these units were more costly to maintain and manage than their higher density, multifamily public housing properties. (Maintenance personnel, for example, had to travel long distances to investigate problems; heating systems, which were not standardized, required special-order parts.)

At the time, it was generally acknowledged that, absent gross mismanagement, scattered-site single-family housing supports a higher quality of life for public housing residents (especially families with children) than do dense high-rise projects. So these individual houses, many of them in nonghetto neighborhoods, were ideal candidates for homeownership.

But a 1985 internal HUD study disputed the widely shared view among public housing authorities that scattered-site housing was more expensive to operate than conventional public housing. According to HUD: "It can be hypothesized that there are operating cost advantages for the typical scattered-site projects—lower vandalism, more tenant care for the units, and more recent construction or major rehabilitation—that out weigh such disadvantages as greater dispersal and fewer economies of scale. . . . When operating receipts are subtracted from total operating costs . . . scattered-site projects almost always show a much smaller operating deficit than comparable non-scattered projects."[3]

It is doubtful that, since 1985, changes in both operating costs and in federal operating-subsidy allocations have dated HUD's findings. There are two more likely explanations of the differences in HUD and local public housing authority perspectives on this matter.

For one thing, while HUD's conclusions are valid for the nation as a whole, they do not necessarily apply to all local public housing authorities. Due to the local politicization of public housing programs, some public housing authorities have suffered declines in management capacities during the past twenty years and are no longer capable of effectively maintaining their large, scattered-site inventories that were acquired during the 1960s.

In addition, HUD used life-cycle costing to reach the conclusion that scattered-site units are less costly than higher-density stock, while public housing authorities were referring to annual operating costs, net of periodic modernization. From the local standpoint, a public housing authority is never guaranteed to receive from HUD enough funds to meet its full operating deficit for that year, let alone all the operating and capital funds it will need to operate and periodically renew the unit over its expected life.

My own view is that scattered-site public housing provides a higher quality of life for public housing families and should not be sold off because of management inefficiencies. Housing authorities that have had trouble managing their single-family inventories typically do a poor job of managing all of their stock. Selling their scattered-site stock does nothing to improve their management capacity and is simply treating a symptom rather than the cause of the problem.

Moreover, if HUD were to move toward a life-cycle approach to funding the full operating and modernization needs of public housing by adding a replacement allowance to the operating-subsidy formula, then public housing authorities would be able to appreciate the same cost-effectiveness of their single-family inventories that HUD has identified. Congress has already directed HUD to move in this direction.

Revitalize Distressed Housing Projects. The Denver Housing Authority tried a different approach. Rather than selling its most desirable scattered-site units, it promoted homeownership in a low-rise multifamily project in a severely depressed neighborhood.

The housing authority first emptied two noncontiguous square-block segments of a large, deteriorating townhouse-type project. It then rehabilitated the units for sale as limited equity co-ops (restrictions would limit the profit that homebuyers are entitled to earn on the resale of their co-op shares). The units were then marketed to public housing families, few of which had previously lived in the project as renters.

Limited experience with co-ops in the Denver community led the public housing authority to seriously underestimate the project's operating requirements—especially local property tax and insurance rates, and the time and resources it would take to prepare these low-income buyers, who had not previously lived together, for effective self-governance and property management. Limited counseling on the responsibilities of home-ownership, little knowledge about how to operate and manage a co-op, and budget shortfalls necessitating unaffordable increases in carrying charges that have been resisted by the homebuyers resulted in problems almost from the start. Both segments of the project have been plagued by high vacancy and turnover rates as well as financial difficulties that make their long-term viability doubtful.

If there is any moral to the Denver experience it is that the allure of homeownership is not strong enough to compel public housing families to accept a bad deal. Multifamily conversions simply will not work unless the quality of rehabilitation is up to homebuyers' expectations, carrying charges do not exceed projections, provisions are made for replacement reserves, and families are adequately counseled about the responsibilities of homeownership and trained in the techniques of cooperative living.

Of course, not all project conversions have been as plagued by problems as this one. A co-op conversion in Nashville, Tennessee, and a condominium project in Louisville, Kentucky (described in detail in Chapter 5), appear to have higher probabilities of long-term success.

Pricing Policies

Under federal law, HUD is authorized to continue paying the debt service associated with original construction and periodic modernization of public housing units to be sold, even after they have been transferred to tenant ownership. But HUD is prohibited from paying operating subsidies on the units once they leave the public housing inventory. To maximize affordability, a public housing authority is permitted to discount the sales price of the house all the way down to zero—to give it away—so that all of the low-income buyer's available resources can be applied to operating costs.

Only a few of the seventeen public housing authorities participating in PHHD chose this pricing strategy. Most took the position that you get what you pay for and don't value what you receive for free. The sales prices usually were established on the basis of appraised value, and then discounted to a level considered affordable to the target population.

Affordability was defined on the basis of a specified housing cost-to-income share—usually between 25 and 35 percent—with local financing arrangements and property tax rates taken into consideration. (That is, holding appraised value and buyer incomes constant, sales prices would be lower where interest rates and local tax rates were higher.)

The average sales price determined by the thirteen public housing authorities that sold at least one unit approached $32,000; the discounted price (which equals the sum of the buyer's down payment and first mortgage) averaged nearly $18,000, or 56 percent of the undiscounted price (see Table 4).

Average undiscounted prices varied significantly from one public housing authority to another. Los Angeles ($87,136) and Washington, D.C. ($64,738), had the highest prices; Muskegon Heights, Michigan ($7,550), and Reading, Pennsylvania ($12,000), had the lowest.

The buyer's first mortgage, averaging slightly over $17,000, was equal to the difference between the discounted sale price and a modest down payment, which averaged less than 3 percent ($841) for all units sold by participating public housing authorities. The difference between the undiscounted and discounted sales price was financed by the public housing authority in the form of a "silent" second mortgage requiring no current debt-service payments. For all units, the silent second mortgage averaged 46 percent of the actual sales price.

Resale Restrictions

Under HUD rules, housing authorities were required to adopt prohibitions against windfall profits from resale for a minimum of five years.

Public housing authorities could extend resale restrictions indefinitely, as those in Denver and Nashville did; they could eliminate them entirely after five years, as those in Newport News, Virginia, and Muskegon Heights, Michigan, did; or they could phase them out over a longer period of time, as in Baltimore, where they were phased out over a ten-year period. Most housing authorities chose this last course.

Most housing authorities enforced HUD's five-year resale restrictions by inserting a repayment provision in the second mortgage loan. Should the buyer sell the unit within the first five years of purchase, the full principal and deferred interest on the second mortgage would be due and payable.

Resale restrictions in Washington, D.C., are very severe for seven years, after which time equity obtained through a sale would be equally shared between the initial buyer and the housing authority. For each additional year after seven years that the original purchaser resides

Table 4
Average Sales Prices
First and Second Mortgage Amounts and Down Payments
for Programs with Sales

Public Housing Authority	Average Sales Price	Average First Mortgage	Average Second Mortgage[a]	Average Down Payment
Baltimore (N=28)	$23,434	$17,649	$ 5,285	$ 500
Chicago (N=14)	22,076	19,789	15,294	2,670[b]
Denver				
Upper Lawrence (N=44)	27,300	18,182	8,500	800[c]
Arapahoe (N=44)	37,500	37,500	0	0
Los Angeles County (N=9)	87,136	35,403	50,463	1,270
McKeesport (N=9)	21,688	18,325	0	3,363[e]
Muskegon Heights (N=2)	7,550	7,200	0	350
Nashville (N=15)	21,177	6,471	14,412	294
Newport News (N=15)	24,213	16,712	7,501	0
Reading (N=8)	12,000	11,400	0	600
St. Mary's County (N=30)	42,500	9,000	32,500	1,000
Tulsa (N=1)	30,000	21,758	7,500	742
Washington, D.C. (N=23)	64,738	17,279	44,220	3,239[f]
Wyoming (N=8)	38,153	21,346	16,167	640
Average (weighted) All Sales	$31,779	$17,097	$14,552	$ 841[g]

N = the number of property sales

a. In all demonstration programs except Denver's Upper Lawrence Co-op, second mortgages are forgiven after a period of time.
b. Sum of mortgages and down payments do not add to sales price because portion of sales proceeds used to rehabilitate the properties is secured by silent second mortgage held by the housing authority.
c. A local nonprofit housing corporation has provided financing for residents who could not meet the down payment requirement.
d. Because Arapahoe is a rental, or conditional sales co-op, sales price is defined as a pro rata share of the first mortgage.
e. The down payments were credit given to purchasers in an amount equal to the previous year's rent payments.
f. Down payments in Washington, D.C., were provided by the city in the form of a silent third mortgage.
g. Excludes closing cost.

Source: William M. Rohe and Michael A. Stegman, *Public Housing Homeownership Demonstration Assessment,* prepared for the U.S. Department of Housing and Urban Development, Washington, D.C., Contract HC-5774, April 1990, p. 62.

in the house, the housing authority's equity share declines by 7 percent. With a current market value of nearly $65,000 and the second mortgage averaging in excess of $44,000, even if property values remain relatively flat in the Capitol Hill neighborhood where Washington's public housing condos are located, the tenants who bought their units under HUD's homeownership demonstration stand to accumulate substantial equity.

HUD's decision not to impose longer resale restrictions has been severely criticized by low-income housing advocates because of severe shortages of affordable housing. It stands in stark contrast to the permanent restrictions imposed by Congress on the resale of units sold to resident management councils in public housing projects under the Housing and Community Development Act. My own view is that resale rules should not be so restrictive that they prevent homebuyers from realizing sufficient equity in their units (due to forgiveness of the second mortgage debt by the public housing authority and/or from market appreciation) that would allow them to enter the unsubsidized market.

Financing with Private Capital

A primary goal of HUD's PHHD was to attract private financing to public housing sales. This effort was successful in just five of the thirteen public housing authorities: three with single-family sales programs (in Wyoming, Michigan; Newport News, Virginia; and Muskegon Heights, Michigan) and two with multifamily programs (Denver, Colorado; and Nashville, Tennessee). Collectively, these five public housing authorities were responsible for the sale of nearly two-thirds of the total number of single and multifamily units that closed during the demonstration period.

Programs targeted to single-family dwellings were less successful in attracting private investment than multifamily co-op conversions. All three multifamily co-ops that closed (two in Denver and one in Nashville), containing a total of 173 units, attracted some private funds; just 35 of the 140 single-family unit sales (25 percent) in the five above-mentioned cities had private financing.

Most private lenders required some form of indemnification, or guaranty against financial loss, in the event of serious delinquency, default, or foreclosure. Thus, even when a sales program included private financing, the public housing authority retained some long-term financial risk.

Indemnification of private lenders participating in the sales of single-family units took several forms—ranging from buying bad loans from banks to buying back foreclosed houses. In Wyoming, Michigan, for example, the public housing authority promised to pay off the outstanding first mortgage in the event that any of its eight homebuyers defaulted on their private loans. In Newport News, Virginia, the public housing authority agreed to buy back, for a period of five years after closing, any bad loan from the minority-owned lending institution that financed the city's fifteen single-family unit sales. The Muskegon Heights, Michigan, public housing authority (which sold only two single-family units) agreed, in the event of foreclosure, to buy the units back from the bank that financed them.

Indemnification of private lenders involved in cooperative conversions was much more complicated. In the case of Denver's forty-four-unit Upper Lawrence cooperative, which was financed in 1987 by loans from the National Consumer Co-op Bank, the Colorado Housing Finance Agency, and a grant from the State Division of Housing, the lenders' protection was indirect. The Denver Housing Authority agreed to acquire the co-op shares of individual buyers who failed to meet their carrying-charge obligations. Because of serious management problems and high turnover rates at Upper Lawrence, the housing authority has already had to make good on this obligation.

The financing of Denver's second co-op, Arapahoe, required even more complicated forms of indemnification because a principal source of funds for the rehabilitation came not from a lender, but from a private investor who demanded protection against risk of loss. In this case, although the public housing authority provided the first mortgage loan, a substantial share of the development cost was raised through the sale (to a wealthy private investor) of low-income housing tax credits generated by substantial rehabilitation of the project. The federal penalty for violation of low-income occupancy and other use restrictions of housing rehabilitated with low-income housing tax credits is recapture of the credits themselves. Thus, in order to attract private capital to the renovation of Arapahoe, the public housing authority had to guarantee the investor against possible future recapture of the tax credits in the event that the cooperative ran afoul of IRS regulations.

Another complicated feature of the financing is the hybrid ownership form of the project. Because, under federal law, low-income housing tax credits can only be used for the acquisition or rehabilitation of rental housing, Arapahoe was structured as a rental co-op in which the residents would not have a direct ownership interest in their units. To form a rental co-op, the public housing authority transfers the project's land to a resident organization (the co-op) and sells the buildings to a partnership consisting of the co-op and the private investor(s). The partnership then rents the buildings to the individual residents at an agreed-upon rental schedule, and agrees to sell the buildings to the co-op at an affordable price when the low-income rental-housing-use restrictions associated with the tax credits expire (at the end of fifteen years when Arapahoe was created; later raised to thirty years by Congress). Thus, at the end of fifteen years, when ownership of the land and buildings is in the hands of the residents, Arapahoe will become a conventional housing cooperative.

Private participation in public housing sales is important because it provides public housing authorities with immediate capital that they can use to finance replacement housing or otherwise enrich their low-income housing programs. But the PHHD experience suggests that, even when it is available, private financing comes with complicated and costly strings, and at interest rates and terms that price the housing out of reach of deserving families. While the PHHD produced some innovative private-financing mechanisms, without federal guarantees or a separate financing program we are not likely to see high-volume public housing sales programs financed through the private lending sector. The one possible exception to this generalization is that we may expect to see greater use of the low-income tax credit to finance public housing conversions if low-income families become more accepting of the concept of a rental co-op that does not give them immediate ownership rights to their buildings.

The Allure of Homeownership

To assess the reasons public housing tenants wanted to own a home, HUD's evaluators asked each buyer a series of multiple-choice questions. The three most frequently cited reasons for wanting to own a home were to be able to fix up the house or yard the way they wanted, to have something to leave to their children, and to have a good financial investment (see Table 5).

But when the buyers were asked to identify the single most important reason for buying, a different pattern emerged. At the top of the list was to have a good financial investment, followed by the desire to have something to leave to their children, and, in third place, to have something to call their own (see Table 5). Thus, both social and economic considerations figured strongly in potential buyers' reasons for wanting to own their homes.

Overall, HUD data indicate that homebuyers' satisfaction with their units was quite high. Over 77 percent of PHHD participants were satisfied; fewer than 10 percent expressed dissatisfaction. Over three-quarters (78 percent) of program participants credited homeownership with feeling better about themselves; more than two-thirds (67 percent)

Table 5
Why Buy?

Participants' Reasons for Buying	Frequency	Percent
To fix up house or yard as wanted	214	78.7
To have something to leave children	200	74.1
To have good financial investment	182	66.9
Most Important Reasons for Buying	**Frequency**	**Percent**
To have good financial investment	71	28.5
To have something to leave children	43	17.3
To have something to call ours	35	14.1

Source: William M. Rohe and Michael A. Stegman, *Public Housing Homeownership Demonstration Assessment,* prepared for the U.S. Department of Housing and Urban Development, Washington, D.C., Contract HC-5774, April 1990, p. 138.

said that homeownership made them feel more financially secure; and over half (52 percent) said that homeownership gave them a greater sense of control over their lives.

The Buyers

Public housing authorities typically screened prospective PHHD participants on the basis of whether the household contained at least one full-time wage earner, their income, and their rent-paying records. Housekeeping practices were also sometimes checked through home visits or recommendations from on-site project managers.

A minimum income was set for participation in the PHHD. The amount was based on the public housing authority's estimate of the resources it would take to cover debt service and operating costs of the units up for sale. Minimum incomes ranged from a low of $7,500 in St. Thomas, Virgin Islands, for the 120-unit Pearson Gardens limited equity co-op, which has yet to close, to a high of $17,000 in Washington, D.C., for Wylie Courts Condominium.

The combination of income, employment, and related eligibility requirements resulted in a composite profile of public housing homebuyers that is strikingly different from that of all public housing residents. For example, in contrast to the national public housing population, where the vast majority of nonelderly tenant households consist of single mothers and their children, nearly half of all tenant-buyers consisted of husband-and-wife families with one or two children (see Table 6).

Another distinction is that 91 percent of households participating in PHHD had at least one full-time wage earner. The average income of these households was $16,673—more than double the national average for all public housing families. In some cities, the incomes of those participating in PHHD were much higher, averaging nearly $24,000 in Newport News, Virginia, and in Washington, D.C.; nearly $23,000 in Los Angeles and in Wyoming, Michigan; more than $19,000 in Baltimore; and more than $20,000 in Chicago.

Because the units that public housing authorities selected for sale tended to be among the best in their inventory and the tenants who bought them had significantly higher incomes than their counterparts, public housing homeownership programs have been criticized for "creaming."

Although the relatively minimal income thresholds required by the public housing authorities for participation in PHHD made a

Table 6
Composition of Participant Households

City	Percentage of Households with One Full-time Employee	Average Household Income	Percentage of Two-Parent Households	Average Household Size
Baltimore (27)*	100.0	$19,000	51.9	3.6
Chicago (15)	93.8	$20,187	87.5	3.8
Denver (71)	93.0	$13,557	50.7	3.6
Los Angeles Co. (9)	100.0	$22,833	88.9	5.2
McKeesport (8)	87.5	$16,625	37.5	4.4
Muskegon Heights (2)	100.0	$19,500	50.0	3.0
Nashville (67)	86.6	$14,008	20.9	2.4
Newport News (11)	81.8	$23,909	81.8	4.3
Paterson (0)	——	——	——	—
Philadelphia	——	——	——	—
Reading (7)	100.0	$11,214	42.9	4.3
St. Mary's Co. (29)	93.1	$16,414	41.4	5.2
Tulsa (0)	——	——	——	—
Washington, D.C. (18)	100.0	$23,389	33.3	4.5
Wichita (0)	——	——	——	—
Wyoming (7)	100.0	$22,786	100.0	5.0
Total Sample	91.3	$16,673	46.7	3.7

*Numbers in parentheses indicate number of buyers.

Source: William M. Rohe and Michael A. Stegman, *Public Housing Homeownership Demonstration Assessment,* prepared for the U.S. Department of Housing and Urban Development, Washington, D.C., Contract HC-5774, April 1990, p. 135.

certain amount of creaming a certainty, minorities were well represented among the homebuyers. In fact, more than 90 percent of all participants were either black (74 percent) or Hispanic (18 percent). (See Table 7.)

Table 7
Racial Composition of PHHD Participants

City	Percent White	Percent Black	Percent Hispanic
Baltimore (27)*	4	96	0
Chicago (15)	0	100	0
Denver (71)	6	44	49
Los Angeles Co. (9)	0	11	89
McKeesport (8)	38	50	12
Muskegon Heights (2)	0	100	0
Nashville (67)	7	93	0
Newport News (11)	0	100	0
Paterson (0)	—	—	—
Philadelphia (0)	—	—	—
Reading (7)	14	29	57
St. Mary's Co. (29)	3	97	0
Tulsa (0)	—	—	—
Washington, D.C. (18)	0	100	0
Wichita (0)	—	—	—
Wyoming (7)	86	0	14
Total Sample	8	74	18

*Numbers in parentheses indicate number of buyers.

Source: William M. Rohe and Michael A. Stegman, *Public Housing Homeownership Demonstration Assessment,* prepared for the U.S. Department of Housing and Urban Development, Washington, D.C., Contract HC-5774, April 1990, p. 135.

Homeowner Satisfaction

While early results suggest a high level of buyer satisfaction, not all buyers will benefit financially or otherwise—as they had hoped—from their flirtation with homeownership.

For one thing, homebuyers' concerns about undesirable and dangerous neighborhood conditions were evident in most cities, running the gamut from dirty, litter-strewn streets (52 percent) to the presence of drugs and drug dealing (58 percent). (See Table 8.) Nearly 30 percent of buyers who bought a public housing unit in a different neighborhood than the one in which they were renting rated their new neighborhood as being in either somewhat worse or much worse condition than their former location. Moreover, 17 percent who bought the same unit they were living in thought that neighborhood conditions worsened during the past year. The latter data suggest that the mere fact of converting tenants to homeowners will do little to improve neighborhood conditions.

For another thing, despite HUD's requirement that all sales units be in good condition before transfer, more than one out of five buyers expressed dissatisfaction with the quality of repairs made to their units prior to sale (see Table 8). While 21 percent of all buyers rated their units as being in excellent condition at the time of closing, over 23 percent judged their units to be in just "fair" condition, and nearly 7 percent rated their units as "poor." Moreover, after closing, when the buyers had assumed major responsibility for maintaining the condition of their units, more than 60 percent indicated that their houses or apartments were in need of additional repairs and renovations.

Serious Delinquencies and Defaults

Long-term affordability is affected by many variables, including the initial sales price and financing terms; the percentage of the buyer's income that the public housing authorities require to be contributed to debt service; local tax and insurance rates; the accuracy of initial multifamily operating budgets (including provisions for reserves); and the extent to which homeowner incomes keep pace with inflation.

Too little time has passed to determine how well former public housing tenants are able to cope with the costs of homeownership. But some data are available that show short-term affordability problems.

To put these numbers in perspective, national figures on homeowner mortgage delinquencies and foreclosures have been provided. The national data are for loan failures as of year-end 1989 for all homeowners who bought modestly priced homes with low-down-payment, FHA-insured loans between 1975 and 1985, which means that all loans were made at least five years ago.

Nationally, default and foreclosure rates are highly associated with initial loan value and the extent of the borrowers' initial equity.[4] Borrowers with low-down-payment loans defaulted on their mortgages five times more frequently than those with higher rates of initial equity.[5] To attach numbers to these rates, nearly 9 percent of all recent FHA-insured loans with an initial down payment of 3 percent or less had failed by the end of 1989, compared to less than 2 percent of all loans with an initial down payment of at least 25 percent.[6]

Table 8
Tenant-Buyer Satisfaction
Neighborhood Problems Perceived by Program Participants

	Number	Percentage
Rundown Buildings	111	40.8
Litter & Garbage	141	51.8
Street Crime	105	38.6
Burglaries	114	42.1
Bothersome People	75	27.7
Drugs & Drug Users	157	57.7
Lack of Adequate Recreation Facilities	136	50.4

Tenant-Buyers' Rating of Condition of Unit Acquired

	Excellent	Good	Fair	Poor
Ratings of Condition of Unit at Closing	21.3%	48.5%	23.5%	6.6%

	Yes	No
Buyers' Perception of Need for Additional Repairs	60.5%	39.5%

Source: William M. Rohe and Michael A. Stegman, *Public Housing Homeownership Demonstration Assessment,* prepared for the U.S. Department of Housing and Urban Development, Washington, D.C., Contract HC-5774, April 1990, pp. 147, 153–54.

Similarly, within the FHA portfolio, lower-valued loans also tended to have a higher rate of default. This was especially true for houses valued under $48,000, where the failure rate was more than 8 percent.[7] This compares, for example, to a foreclosure rate of around 5 percent on higher-valued loans.

Early evidence on homeowner delinquency and default in PHHD indicates that five out of the demonstration's thirteen programs that closed at least one sale experienced problems with late payments or more serious delinquencies. HUD's PHHD evaluators confirmed that 10 to 15 percent of the buyers experienced some problems meeting their housing costs within the first eighteen months after closing on their home.[8] About 31 percent of all PHHD homebuyers indicated in interviews that their mortgage payments were causing a strain on their budgets, and 10 percent said they were in arrears on their payments by at least one month.

Loss rates could be in the same range. This raises the question of what failure rate is morally, politically, and financially acceptable in a program that sells public housing residents their units at deeply discounted prices, but provides no continuing subsidies. My own view is that losses in the 10 percent range are unacceptable on all three counts.

It is important to examine the causes of default. According to theory and most empirical studies, "Default is most likely to occur when a borrower has a negative equity position in the property—normally because the value of the property has fallen below the loan balance."[9] (Equity equals the difference between market value and the discounted price the buyer actually paid.) Simply stated, when a housing market is depressed and prices fall, homeowners (especially those with little of their own cash invested in their house) may be able to maximize their wealth by walking away from their property rather than continuing to make their mortgage payments.

During the late 1970s, for example, when house price appreciation across the country ran around 12 percent a year, default rates were very low.[10] Since 1980, house prices have increased by less than 3 percent a year, and default rates have soared.[11]

This theory applies directly to the PHHD. If a homeowner has a substantial amount of net equity in her property, even if she suffers a job or other personal reversal and can no longer afford to meet her housing payments, her rational course of action would be to sell rather than to walk away from her property. This means that a high incidence of financial stress among public housing homeowners does not automatically translate into a high rate of foreclosure. But, if sales programs are structured in such a way that the financially strapped buyer has little or no equity in her property, chances are enhanced that she will take a walk when the going gets rough. Early experiences with Denver's PHHD projects support this proposition.

Denver's two separate public housing cooperatives required little upfront cash from buyers, and what little initial equity they began with was quickly dissipated due to a combination of management and other problems. As a result, within eighteen months of closing, one of the coops had a 20 percent delinquency rate, and a third of all buyers in the other were behind in their housing payments. Moreover, annual turnover in the more troubled co-op was around 27 percent. And virtually all of this turnover occurred without the sale of a single co-op share ever having taken place. At least among these public housing resident-buyers—Jack Kemp's sentiments notwithstanding that "owning something changes behavior in ways that no amount of preaching middle-class values ever could"[12]—around one in five low-income families has already walked away from their public housing co-ops as if they were renters. This brings us back to the proposition that most defaults occur when a borrower's equity is negative.

In contrast to most single-family demonstration programs, in which sales prices were based on market appraisals and then discounted to affordable levels, in two out of the three multifamily conversions that went to closing, sales prices were based on rehabilitation costs. From day one, single-family homebuyers have a positive equity position in their property. If they remain in their homes beyond the expiration of public-housing-authority-imposed resale restrictions, they will be able to realize the full amount of their initial equity by selling or refinancing their property. If property values appreciate during their tenure, so will the value of their equity.

This is not the case in multifamily ownership projects, in which the price of a co-op share is set not by a market appraisal but at a pro rata share of the cost of rehabilitating the property. Rather than reflecting real equity that the buyer can eventually realize if she takes care of her unit, the forgivable silent second mortgage held by the public housing authority merely represents excess debt that the buyers cannot afford to pay off on a monthly basis. Given their negative equity positions from the day the co-op closes, it is not surprising to find buyers taking a walk when there are unforeseen changes in their personal circumstances, when the enormity of the responsibility sets in, or when mismanagement of the co-op leads to deteriorating operating conditions.

There are two policy implications that can be gleaned from Denver's early experiences in the PHHD. First, as long as there is going to be a public housing homeownership program, families should be given a positive equity stake in their property from the very beginning. Since the buyers are unable to make large down payments, resale restrictions and prohibitions against windfall profits should be liberalized so that families can realize their locked-in equity more quickly. Second, even with deeply discounted prices, many families are going to require continuing subsidies in order to be able to afford their housing. While some privatization proponents might see this as perpetuating the dependency relationship that the sale of public housing is supposed to end, the alternative is to let as many as one out of ten buyers slip through the safety net.

Nonbuyers

HUD's guidelines explicitly prohibited involuntary relocation of tenants who were unable or unwilling to participate in the sales program. In accordance with this guideline, most public housing authorities simply did not sell single-family units occupied by families who did not qualify for, or were not interested in, participation in the program. But in multifamily sites, public housing authorities took a more aggressive approach, offering nonbuyers enticements to move—such as Section 8 certificates, housing vouchers, or other public housing units— and the option of remaining in their rental units as tenants of the newly formed cooperatives.

But as the following experience in Denver suggests, when it comes to differentiating between incentives and pressures to move, the perceptions of nonbuyers and the public housing authority can be quite different.

During the course of the PHHD, a total of 136 nonbuying households occupying multifamily units were relocated to other units; 128 of these were in Denver's two co-ops, where entire buildings were vacated to allow for extensive modernization.

HUD's PHHD evaluators interviewed thirty-four of the sixty-four families relocated in conjunction with the creation of the Upper Lawrence co-op in Denver. Almost three-quarters of these families had incomes below $5,000; only 12 percent had incomes over $8,000, which is far below the $12,000 minimum income required for joining the co-op. Moreover, in only 18 percent of the families was there one or more persons with full-time employment; 90 percent were single-parent households. A total of 65 percent of the relocatees interviewed said their move was involuntary.

Regulations clearly prohibit housing authorities from forcing out families that do not qualify to buy their apartments. HUD should now create an appeals mechanism for families that believe that, despite these regulations, they are not being treated fairly. (For example, there are families that believe they are being moved for no other purpose than to promote the sale of their project.)

Litigation on Involuntary Relocation

Notwithstanding residents' complaints that they were being "forced" to move, Denver's two co-ops proceeded without the threat of, or actual, litigation. This was not the case in Paterson, New Jersey, where legal proceedings brought the public housing homeownership demonstration to a virtual halt. Although Paterson was the only PHHD site where the issue of relocating nonbuyers was litigated, the implications of the settlement reach beyond the city's borders.

It was hoped that when the 242-unit Brooks-Sloate Terrace Apartments in Paterson, New Jersey, were converted into a limited-equity cooperative, the tenants who occupied the public housing project would become the 242 shareholders. But some families, of course, were too poor to join the co-op, and others were not interested in buying their apartments.

To meet these contingencies, and to conform to HUD regulations, the original program provided that "residents who do not choose to buy or who cannot afford the carrying costs will either be transferred to other housing authority developments or, if qualified, will be given vouchers that will allow them to rent housing from private sources."

It was never envisioned that a sizable number of nonbuying families would remain in their apartments as tenants of the Brooks-Sloate Co-op. But that is exactly what happened as part of a settlement in a legal action against HUD and the public housing authority over the issue of involuntary relocation.

The legal action, *Frierson v. Pierce et al.*, was filed in the United States District Court in New Jersey in October 1988 on behalf of tenants then living in Brooks-Sloate apartments, a low-income family on the waiting list for public housing in Paterson, and the Paterson Coalition for Housing, Inc. (an organization that helps homeless people find apartments). The plaintiffs challenged the validity of HUD's PHHD regulations that required only a five-year limit on resale of public housing units to low-income families because this meant that beginning in year six, the former public housing units could be sold at market prices—which are beyond the reach of the poor. The plaintiffs also charged that the plan to transfer nonbuying tenants to other public housing developments or to provide them with housing vouchers constituted involuntary relocation, which frustrated the purpose of the National Housing Act and was prohibited by PHHD regulations.

The plaintiffs' third complaint was that New Jersey's Cause for Eviction Statute had been violated. The statute requires that "tenants be provided with a 60 day 'notice' and a three (3) year Notice to Quit before eviction proceedings may be commenced against the tenant. Within the first 18 months of that three-year period, the tenant has the option of demanding of the landlord comparable rental housing. If the landlord does not provide comparable rental housing, the tenant is entitled to stays of eviction for up to five (5) years beyond the first three (3) years."

According to the plaintiffs, the public housing authority failed to provide any of these required notices.

On July 18, 1989, a settlement was reached among the parties to the litigation. The settlement prohibits the public housing authority from involuntary relocation of tenants of Brooks-Sloate apartments. According to the settlement, "This means that tenants may not be moved, and threatened with being moved, against their will from their present dwelling units." "Involuntary relocation" does not encompass offering a tenant the choice of accepting a Section 8 certificate, voucher, or another public housing unit. The settlement also makes clear that the failure to supply a housing voucher to any Brooks-Sloate resident who wishes to remain as a tenant of the co-op shall be considered the equivalent of involuntary relocation.

Major Problems and Constraints

The Public Housing Homeownership Demonstration officially commenced on June 5, 1985, when HUD Secretary Samuel R. Pierce first made public the names of the seventeen participating public housing authorities. But it did not end, as planned, thirty-six months later. In fact, the majority of public housing units sold actually closed after the official thirty-six-month demonstration period. The last day of HUD's on-site data-collection effort—September 1, 1989—more accurately reflects the ending of the sales period, which was a few days short of fifty-one months. Clearly, HUD and the participating public housing authorities underestimated the time and effort it would take to design and implement this program.

Overall, title was transferred to 320 public housing units, just a quarter of the 1,315 units HUD had hoped would be sold. Sales varied greatly from one site to another. Six of the seventeen public housing authorities, for example, achieved 90 percent or more of their sales goals, including four that sold all units offered. At the same time, eight public housing authorities achieved less than 15 percent of their sales goals or sold no units at all. More significant than the disappointing sales numbers is the fact that demand for buying these units was so low among public housing tenants that, despite HUD's requirement that sales had to be made to public housing tenants, nearly one out of four sales was to nonresident households on public housing waiting lists.

Public housing authorities' failure to carry out their homeownership demonstrations at the scale and pace originally intended, or, in some cases, to carry them out at all, was the result of ineffective management or commitment; conflict within the community over the goals of the sales program; flawed program design; adverse local market conditions; inadequate tenant incomes; and lack of replacement housing.

Ineffective Management and/or Commitment. Several demonstration programs faltered because the public housing authority or local governing body simply was not committed to the program. In some cases, this was because new public housing authority directors had been hired or new board members had been appointed who were not supportive of PHHD; in other cases, the public housing authority had to focus on more pressing problems.

Major management problems within the Philadelphia Housing Authority almost killed what was intended to be HUD's largest public housing homeownership demonstration program. Initially targeted to sell three hundred single-family units, this sales program did not even materialize during the thirty-six-month demonstration period. Despite more than 7,000 scattered-site units in inventory, the program was foiled by insufficient commitment of time and high-level staff, lack of clear staff responsibility for the sales program, and disagreement over replacement housing. Within the past year, under new leadership, a fifteen-unit pilot program has been designed, and buyers are now being selected.

In Chicago, similar management problems also led to disappointing results. While Chicago's sales goal was more modest—thirty-one single-family units—it reached less than 50 percent of its goal, selling only fourteen.

One reason for poor performance by the Chicago public housing authority was that its homeownership program director left and no new director was appointed; administration was left up to a public housing authority attorney. Another reason was that the staff members who designed the demonstration left the public housing authority midway through its implementation. Still another reason was the lack of funds for financial counseling of prospective buyers, who were ill-equipped to secure the necessary mortgages by themselves.

Interviews with local program officials revealed that many of the demonstration programs were understaffed. This was particularly true in the case of multifamily housing sales programs, but it also was the case in some single-family housing programs.

In part, the public housing authorities, which lacked experience with homeownership programs, simply underestimated the amount of staff time that would be required. In part, the staff assigned to the demonstration had other responsibilities related to the primary activity of their agencies—that is, managing public housing.

In many instances, those in charge of PHHD had to rely on staff from other departments within the public housing authority for assistance with such matters as conducting inspections or arranging for rehabilitation of the units; these staff members did not always fully cooperate because of their own work load or because they did not agree with the idea of selling public housing.

Combined with staff turnover, reorganizations within the public housing authorities, and the fact that the majority of public housing authorities had no experience with homeownership programs, the staff assigned to design and manage the programs had much to learn.

Conflict within the Community. Community divisiveness over the Muskegon Heights public housing homeownership program brought the program to a complete standstill. HUD had approved the public housing authority's request to sell twenty single-family scattered-site units at half of their appraised value (in the $15,000–$20,000 range). The public housing authority had closed two sales at an average price of $7,550 when local elections changed the composition of the city council.

Although the mayor of Muskegon Heights continued to support the program, the newly elected council did not. A debate ensued over who held title to the public housing. If the legal title to public housing was vested in the city, then the city council, not the housing authority, could determine the conditions under which the stock could be sold—including the sales price. The dispute was resolved in favor of the city council, which doubled the sales price by voting to sell the public housing at full appraised value.

Flawed Program Design. Miscalculation and poor program design decisions also led to failure. In Wichita, for example, the public housing authority decided to sell its poorest-quality stock (fifty scattered-site units) at the highest possible price—without rehabilitating the properties.

Assuming that it could attract buyers and private lenders to finance the sales, the public housing authority intended to allocate a portion of the sales proceeds to help the new homeowners rehabilitate their units through a combination of sweat equity and housing-authority-sponsored work; another portion of the sales proceeds would be used to subsidize the financing costs of market-rate loans. But HUD rejected the plan because it violated the requirement that all housing transferred to residents be in good condition.

Adverse Local Market Conditions. A soft housing market also undermined the efforts of one public housing authority's participation in PHHD. Tulsa's public housing authority, which hoped to sell one hundred scattered-site single-family homes, was able to market only one unit.

The plan was a generous one. The public housing authority would sell the units at 75 percent of their appraised value, using Federal Housing Administration-insured market-rate financing. No down payment would be required, and a one-year lease/purchase arrangement would allow buyers to accumulate $25 a month toward closing costs if they maintained their units during the lease period.

But at the same time that the Tulsa public housing authority began its sales program, the Federal Housing Administration offered its local HUD-held inventory of 1,500 single-family homes to prospective buyers at even more generous terms—including the use of liberalized underwriting standards to qualify buyers.

As a result, Tulsa's public housing authority participation in PHHD was a failure. Although Tulsa was the only public housing homeownership demonstration to have been thwarted by an excessive supply of other government-owned affordable housing, large inventories of Federal Housing Administration–foreclosed properties in many other cities should act as a constraint on the program's expansion. In fact, HUD has announced plans to mount a national demonstration to sell 1,500 Federal Housing Administration–held single-family properties to state and local governments and nonprofit organizations for resale to low-income families.[13]

As soon as it reaches 1,500 sales, HUD plans to convert this to a permanent program, which will compete with public housing sales programs for the relatively few tenants who can qualify for homeownership. But selling Federal Housing Administration–foreclosed properties at deep discounts makes more sense than doing the same with public housing. While the public housing units slated for sale were originally built and/or purchased to provide low-income families with rental housing at permanently affordable prices, Federal Housing Administration–held inventory, which currently sits vacant, was built for private ownership; the longer it sits vacant, the higher the government's holding costs and the more likely it will be vandalized and blight the neighborhood. It makes better policy sense to sell the Federal Housing Administration–held inventory to qualified public housing residents than it does to sell public housing; this way, the vacated public housing unit becomes available for a poorer family on the waiting list.

Inadequate Tenant Incomes. Since pricing policies were left entirely up to local discretion, a public housing authority could maximize sales by lowering prices enough to make units affordable. But even if the properties were given away, the buyer would still have to have a high enough income to pay full operating costs. Although discounts as high as 100 percent were permissible, for a variety of reasons, no public housing authority chose to give away its houses.

In general, prices were on the high side. When asked why they set their prices as high as they did, some public housing authorities said that they wanted to generate revenues to reinvest in additional housing; others indicated that "if you give it away, the buyer will treat it as if it has no value."

Some public housing authorities, like those in Denver and Nashville, priced their units to recover rehabilitation costs. This meant that buyers would have to be able to pay for a certain amount of debt service in addition to full operating costs. In most programs, though, rehabilitation costs were financed in other ways.

Most housing authorities set their prices at market value and then discounted them to affordable levels. This meant that the sales prices of identical houses varied with the incomes of the buyers, but that virtually all buyers assumed some mortgage debt. In general, first mortgage amounts were based on the amount of debt that buyers could carry, given mortgage terms and a 25 to 30 percent housing expense-to-income ratio. On average, the first mortgage burden on homeowners was nearly $17,100. By insisting that the homebuyer assume some mortgage debt, the public housing authorities increased the minimum-income requirements of potential homebuyers and thereby limited sales potential.

Because public housing authorities could vary sales prices depending upon the income of the potential buyer, income constraints were more likely to affect the pace and extent of housing sales than they were to keep the program from getting off the ground. Still, barring new financing arrangements or dramatic changes in pricing policies, inadequate tenant incomes may well limit the expansion of these programs.

Lack of Replacement Housing. HUD did not require the public housing authorities participating in PHHD to replace the housing they sold, but neither would HUD provide funds for replacement housing. As a result, a number of public housing authorities proposed fewer properties for sale than they would have had funds for replacement housing been available. Moreover, due to the public housing authorities' inability to resolve the problem of nonbuyers in multifamily properties slated for conversion, progress was significantly slowed. Two such projects, in St. Thomas and Paterson, may never go to closing because of conflicts over the replacement-housing issue.

In general, most participating public housing authorities have indicated an unwillingness to expand their sales efforts, now that the demonstration period has ended, unless HUD provides funds for replacement housing.

Even if the limited number of sales that took place during the demonstration period is attributed to a slower-than-anticipated start-up and a longer-than-anticipated learning curve, the PHHD was a disappointment. The record is disappointing for many reasons. Among them: private financing could be secured only when public housing authorities were willing to assume the lenders' risk of loss; selling public housing is an enormously labor-intensive process that, in light of most housing authorities' staffing constraints, could not be accommodated; public housing authorities were not prepared to offer residents the counseling and training necessary to maximize their chances of becoming successful homeowners; resident incomes limited the size of the home-ownership market; despite deep price discounts, some buyers were having a hard time meeting their housing payments; and the process of converting multifamily public housing projects to cooperative ownership was complicated by the fact that large numbers of residents were either not interested or too poor to buy their apartments.

RESIDENT MANAGEMENT COUNCILS

About the same time that the Reagan administration was putting together the broad outlines of its national Public Housing Homeownership Demonstration(PHHD), conservative Republican congressman Jack Kemp was floating his own ideas in the House of Representatives on how the privatization of public housing should proceed. A long-standing critic of what he saw as heavily centralized, inefficient, and insensitive public housing authority management, an enthusiastic supporter of tenant management, and a booster of opportunity capitalism, Kemp introduced his own privatization bill that featured a Thatcher-like right to buy through tenant associations.

Kemp's idea was to sell entire projects to tenant associations, which would then sell units to individual families. The sales price of individual units would be set at 25 percent of market value, and sales would be financed by public housing authorities at an interest rate of 70 percent of the going market rate. Kemp also held that individual tenants should have the right to buy their units even if the rest of the project was not sold. It was this right-to-buy provision that brought resistance to his initiative.

While the Kemp measure garnered substantial support in the House, the right-to-buy provision raised serious concerns both in the Senate and in HUD. Senator William Proxmire, then chair of the Senate Housing

Subcommittee, wrote on August 14, 1986, that public housing authorities hold title to public housing under the National Housing Act, and
that "Congress cannot require local housing authorities to sell assets which
they own."[14] HUD basically agreed, responding that "it appears there
could be a substantial legal risk in attempting sales without PHA con-
sent. . . . Even if [HUD] were to succeed in a legal challenge, the disar-
ray and delay attendant to defending the legislation could frustrate successful homeownership ventures. . . ." HUD recommended, instead,
promoting "a partnership involving HUD, PHAs, resident management corporations, and individual tenant purchasers."[15]

Kemp's original measure did not become law, but a variant of it—minus
the right-to-buy provision—was enacted by Congress as Section 123 of
the Housing and Community Development Act of 1987. Section 123 provides for the sale of multifamily public housing projects to qualifying
Resident Management Councils (RMCs), which are then permitted to
resell individual units to tenants.

At the time the act was passed, there were probably fewer than twenty resident management councils in existence with any actual management
experience. Only a handful met Section 123's requirement that a resident management council had to have at least three years of management experience in order to buy its project. Therefore, to expand sales
potential, Kemp substantially expanded HUD funding of new resident
management groups. There are now more than one hundred operational
resident management councils.

Nevertheless, even if fifty new resident management groups in projects averaging 250 units were to receive HUD training funds each year
(twice the rate of Kemp's tenant management support in fiscal years 1989
and 1990), less than 20 percent of all public housing units in the nation
would be eligible to be sold under Section 123 fifteen years from now.
And this assumes that all resident groups receiving training funds will
mature to the point of demonstrating three years of management
excellence—the standard used in Section 123 to determine eligibility
for ownership transfer.

What Resident Management Entails

Basically, tenant management involves the election of a board of
directors from among the tenants themselves, and the training of that
board in organizational skills and in the principles and practices of
real estate management. Generally, routine daily management in
tenant-managed projects is carried out by staff hired from the resident
population.

David Caprara and Bill Alexander estimated that to achieve competency, tenants participating in resident management require more than a thousand hours of formal training in, among other things, community organization and institutional development (creating a viable resident management council), the fundamentals of business and property management, and public housing modernization—as well as homeownership counseling.[16]

As indicated above, until 1988, HUD did not provide funding to train and otherwise assist tenant management councils in developing the skills they need to handle their responsibilities at expected levels of competence. But HUD planned to create training programs for resident management and homeownership transfer. According to the department, "Regional training programs will be conducted for program participants in all ten HUD regions in the coming year [1990], with emphasis on financial management and program compliance."[17]

While resident management generates additional employment opportunities and such benefits as a sense of personal development, the most systematic empirical analysis undertaken to date (1980) indicates that it also incurs significant additional costs. Resident management costs from 13 percent to 62 percent more than traditional management, primarily because of the additional paid tenant-staff hired to deliver a wide variety of services that were not being provided by the public housing authority.[18] While advocates of resident management argue that today's better-trained resident management councils will cost less than conventional management because of greater efficiencies and cooperation from residents, no empirical studies have yet confirmed this belief.

Stimulating Tenant Participation

To stimulate tenant participation in resident management councils, HUD requires public housing authorities to inform their tenants about resident participation opportunities, to determine their interest in forming a tenant organization, and to assist in the establishment of such an organization. Until recently, there was no special funding to support such tenant activities. But in 1988, Kemp made resources available to resident management councils by reallocating existing HUD funds.

In fiscal 1988, HUD awarded technical assistant grants totaling $2.5 million to twenty-seven public housing authorities, resident organizations, and resident management councils to fund activities associated with resident management. In fiscal 1989, another $2.5 million was made available for this purpose, with the qualification that no more than $100,000 be approved for any single public housing project.[19] The administration's fiscal 1991 budget proposes more money—$96 million—for resident management initiatives, which would grow to $260 million in 1992 and $400 million in 1993. Congress also acted to strengthen resident management initiatives in the 1987 Housing and Community Development Act by allowing resident management councils to retain revenues earned in excess of operating costs.

In general, the larger the public housing authority the more likely it is to embrace tenant participation. About 50 percent of all large (1,251 to 2,500 units) and 72 percent of all very large (2,501 or more units) public housing authorities have formed resident management councils, compared to just 15 percent of all small (1 to 500 units) public housing authorities.

While, to date, most of the interest in resident management has occurred in large, deteriorated projects operated by large and very large public housing authorities, this fact should not discourage advocates of resident management from promoting resident management in smaller public housing authorities. For one thing, larger public housing authorities are more likely to have formal arrangements with tenants to allow tenants to take over various maintenance and tenant-services responsibilities, and to hire tenants on the public housing authority staff—although such arrangements are not very widespread. Still, it should be noted that the vast majority—87 percent—of public housing authorities are small (operating fewer than 500 units), in which resident management has been less evident.

The Kenilworth-Parkside Resident Management Corporation

To support its position that tenant management provides "significant economic and social benefits, such as reducing the cost of operating public housing, reducing vandalism, and increasing the stake residents have in their housing," HUD has cited the results of a management audit it commissioned of a single tenant management enterprise in Washington, D.C.: the Kenilworth-Parkside Resident Management Corporation.[20]

But the General Accounting Office has questioned HUD's empirical support for this privatization initiative. In a report published in December 1989, the General Accounting Office concluded that "due to a lack of data," HUD's audit "did not contain sufficient information to rule out the possibility that most of the benefits attributed to tenant management might have occurred in its absence."[21]

Built in 1959, Kenilworth-Parkside is a 464-unit public housing development located in northwest Washington, D.C. From 1975 to 1982, the project was managed by Central City Property Management, a minority-owned private management firm that was unable to stop the project's decline. According to the *Washington Times,* during this period "the residents, the majority of whom were single women with children and 85 percent of whom received welfare assistance, felt powerless and embattled. Residents lived three years without heat and hot water. Criminals came and went as they pleased."[22]

The situation at Kenilworth-Parkside changed radically when a tenant committee, determined to turn things around, formed a resident management council and successfully petitioned Washington, D.C., mayor Marion Barry for permission to repair and maintain the property. "A sense of community quickly developed in the old battle zone. . . . Individuals did renovations and repairs," and, by 1984, the Kenilworth-Parkside environment had improved significantly. The change had "reduced teenage pregnancies by 50 percent, reduced welfare dependency by 50 percent, reduced crime by 75 percent, increased rent receipts 130 percent . . . administrative costs were cut by 64 percent during the first year of operation by hiring residents to perform maintenance. . . . Kenilworth Parkside now generates enough revenue to absorb all of its operating expenses."[23]

Kenilworth-Parkside's accomplishments—as well as those in Bromley-Heath in Boston, in Carr Square Village and Cochran Gardens in St. Louis, and in several other resident-managed projects—support Caprara and Alexander's proposition that "when resident management is under the stewardship of dynamic, aggressive leaders, stunning results are achieved."[24] But in each case, only anecdotal evidence, not systematic empirical research, has been cited to confirm the effectiveness of resident management.

That anecdotal evidence, much of it presented in books and articles written by individuals affiliated with the National Center for Neighborhood Enterprise, stands in stark contrast to an independent evaluation of HUD's own $20 million national tenant management demonstration.

HUD's Tenant Management Demonstration Program

HUD's tenant management demonstration program was carried out on seven sites from 1977 to 1979. Only one of the seven tenant management corporations that participated in that demonstration still exists—the Iroquois Resident Management Council—and the Housing Authority of Louisville, Kentucky, recently terminated its contract on the grounds of poor performance.

According to outside consultants, who evaluated the Iroquois Management Council's handling of the 853-unit family development, the Iroquois resident management council fared worse on six measures of management effectiveness than did the managers of two control projects.[25] Vacancy rates, rent arrearages, labor grievances, and the number of days not worked by maintenance department employees were all significantly higher in the resident-managed project. In addition, maintenance conditions were worse, in part because the Iroquois resident management council was unable to hire enough maintenance employees from the development to keep up with demands, and many of those who were hired were poorly trained and insufficiently motivated.[26]

The evaluators also found very low rates of resident participation in resident management council elections, a general unwillingness to serve on the policymaking board, and a self-perpetuating coterie of people who ran the affairs at Iroquois and benefited "in material ways"— such as the allocation of larger-than-needed apartments or day-care center jobs—unanticipated by the public housing authority when the experiment began.[27]

That Iroquois was the resident-managed project that was second-longest-lived of the seven that participated in HUD's demonstration, yet was terminated for poor performance after nearly ten years of operation, shows why we should not evaluate ongoing processes like resident management over a two- to three-year period. Nevertheless, policymakers are reluctant to wait much longer than this for a bottom-line answer on impact and cost-effectiveness. Thus, the Manpower Development Research Corporation's formal evaluation of the HUD demonstration was able to monitor the operations of the seven resident management councils for just three years—from 1977 to 1979.

On the basis of this three-year assessment, the Manpower Development Research Corporation concluded that "at least in the short run, tenant management does not usually produce results markedly superior to those stemming from conventional housing authority management."[28] The Manpower Development Research Corporation further concluded that "tenant management was not significantly better than housing authority management in terms of individual performance indicators such as average rent collections, vacancy rates, or speed or response to maintenance requests."[29]

Overall, the Manpower Development Research Corporation found that resident management generally did not pay for itself in operating costs or other economies. It concluded that "it would be unwise to mandate tenant management of public housing—either requiring it everywhere or prohibiting it everywhere. Rather, individual housing authorities should be able to pursue it if they desire, and if they meet certain preconditions. *HUD should act as a sympathetic respondent to an interest in tenant management expressed locally if it has enough resources to help local housing authorities finance the additional costs involved."* [emphasis added][30]

While HUD continues to assert the cost-reducing benefits of tenant management, even its own inspector general concedes that too much of the evidence is anecdotal. Moreover, he acknowledges that even within the small body of more scientific research, "most of the existing evaluation data in support of the effectiveness of public housing resident management and homeownership are incomplete and conflicting."[31]

HUD's inspector general has called for more systematic, independent evaluations of existing initiatives, while suggesting that the department implement "cost/benefit analyses of the public housing resident management and homeownership programs to ensure that efficient and effective strategies are being employed in these programs and at a reasonable cost to the Federal Government."[32]

The Importance of Tenant Selection

Effective July 15, 1988, HUD directed all local housing authorities to implement, and give precedence to, federal tenant-selection criteria over local selection procedures. The HUD criteria gave priority to income-eligible applicants on waiting lists for public housing who were either involuntarily displaced, living in substandard housing, or paying more than 50 percent of their family income for rent.

This is the latest effort by HUD and Congress—an effort strenuously opposed by public housing authorities—to target public housing to the poorest and worst off, effectively making public housing authorities housers of last resort. Public housing authorities' objections to this latest HUD directive are largely based on the belief that it is not possible to maintain healthy public housing communities without more working families with higher incomes. The combination of the congressional requirement that new occupants of public housing be very poor (below 50 percent of the local median income) and HUD's tenant-selection preferences means that public housing authorities are no longer able to create socioeconomically balanced communities.

But not all local housing authorities adhered to the HUD directive. The Cochran Gardens Resident Management Corporation in St. Louis, for example, used a highly subjective and possibly discriminatory system to select its tenants.

Applicants seeking admission to Cochran Gardens were screened and rated by a resident selection committee. The process included evaluation of marital status (if a marriage appeared stable, the score was 3; if unstable, 0); employment status (steady employment scored 3; employable persons not seeking employment scored 0); quality of child care (if the applicant handled his/her own situation or hired an adequate baby-sitter, the score was 3; if the baby-sitter was under eighteen, the score was 2; if there was no steady baby-sitter and no authority was given to the baby-sitters used, the score was 1; if the children were left alone, the score was 0). The general impression given by the applicant also was scored. If the applicant impressed the selection committee as all talk, not much action, rude, hard to get along with, alcoholic, etc., he/she received a score of 2, 1, 0 accordingly.[33] Despite the fact that Cochran Gardens is one of the two most successful resident-managed developments in the country, under current law, no housing authority in the country is allowed to screen and score applicants in this way.

HUD's inspector general asked HUD's own Office of Fair Housing and Equal Opportunity to review the Cochran Gardens tenant-selection system. In October 1989, it reported that "final selection is totally subjective. . . . When impressions of people are used rather than definitive methods, disparate treatment frequently comes into play, thus leaving the door wide open for discrimination."[34]

In defending its screening process, the Cochran Gardens leadership showed why resident selection for public housing is an issue that must be elevated to the highest level of national policy consideration: "The Cochran Gardens RMC . . . recognized that some households had serious financial and social problems that would adversely affect other residents of the project [and] *contended that the social services and related funding necessary to assist these households did not exist either at the PHA or RMC.*"[35] [emphasis added]

Rather than acknowledging that resident selection is a critical issue for all assisted housing, the inspector general's response to the problem has been to encourage HUD to exempt resident-managed public housing from HUD's tenant-selection policies.[36] For HUD to do so, while praising the effectiveness of resident management and condemning the ineffectiveness of conventionally managed public housing, would be highly irresponsible.

What HUD should do is work with its Office of Fair Housing and Equal Opportunity to create a tenant-selection system that balances the equities between public housing residents struggling to maintain a safe, secure, and peaceful residential environment and those seeking housing, while keeping purely subjective selection criteria to an absolute minimum. The most important lesson from the Cochran Gardens experience is not that resident management councils discriminate, but that strict tenant screening is a prerequisite to success. The Cochran Gardens leadership was also acutely aware that public housing authorities forced to accept families with severe social problems into their projects without the resources to treat them will inevitably end up failing not only those families but the rest of the public housing community.

The Politics of Privatization

Without question, the endorsement of resident management by the Reagan and Bush administrations has muddied the housing policy waters for liberal supporters of self-help housing who have generally been supportive of programs that advocate more rather than less community control. This is because New Right advocates have begun to link the privatization of public housing to resident management, which is making it increasingly difficult to support one without the other.

The National Center for Neighborhood Enterprise, for example, a conservative research and advocacy organization, believes that "when residents become managers and owners and acquire an equity stake in their residences and, in turn, their neighborhoods, they have a reason to change their behavior from destructive to constructive, as well as the incentives to encourage their neighbors to operate and maintain their property."[37]

Robert Woodson, president of the National Center for Neighborhood Enterprise, raised $1.9 million from the Amoco Foundation to provide "education, training and technical assistance to public housing residents to assist them in establishing resident management corporations within the public housing sites in which they live, *a first step toward ownership and privatization.*"[38] [emphasis added]

Liberals who favor more resident control but oppose privatization have been forced into a political corner. They cannot support further allocations for resident management because successful resident management programs would only increase the likelihood of a wholesale public housing sales program down the line.

Gordon Cavanaugh, spokesman for the Council of Large Public Housing Authorities, is a leading proponent of the view that resident management is the New Right's vehicle for getting the federal government out of the low-income housing business. According to Cavanaugh,

"The conservative agenda is ending public ownership of public housing, and they cloak that agenda in the rhetoric of empowerment."[39]

A Comparison of PHHD and Section 123

While the PHHD was designed to help individual public housing
tenants to become homeowners (through the direct sale of single-
family houses and apartments to public housing residents), Section 123
was created first to sell whole projects to resident organizations—that
is, to privatize public housing—and only secondarily to create homeownership opportunities for individuals. Under the PHHD, the transition to homeownership occurs in one step. Under Section 123, homeownership is a two-step process in which the time between the two steps is
indeterminate.

Under Section 123, the title to a multifamily project is first transferred
to a resident management council—at which time the public housing
resident becomes a tenant of the resident management council. This
is supposed to be an interim step toward homeownership. The second
step is when the resident management council transfers title to the project to a cooperative corporation in which the tenants acquire stock and
thus become homeowners. But Section 123 neither provides the resident
management council resources to facilitate this latter step nor sets a time
limit for completion of the conversion to individual-unit ownership.

Thus, public housing residents who live in projects slated for Section
123 transfers enter an interim status of unknown duration on their way
to homeownership—a status in which their rights as public housing tenants (including security of tenure and receipt of operating subsidies to
keep their housing affordable) are less certain than before. Operating
as landlords, resident management councils are much less accountable
to HUD and to the public than are public housing authorities.

Both PHHD and Section 123 prohibit the eviction of tenants who either
are not interested in buying, or are unable to buy, their units. But this
is where the similarity of treatment of nonbuyers ends. PHHD rules require
public housing authorities to come up with incentives to encourage nonbuyers to move to other public or private housing, or, in the case of a
multifamily cooperative or condominium conversion, to accommodate
them in the properties once sold. This includes providing nonpartici-
pating families with Section 8 certificates or vouchers so that they can
continue to rent from the cooperative.

Section 123 provisions on nonbuyers are much more protective of
their rights—although it is not clear how these rights will be secured nor
the route through which tenant grievances (such as harassment) will

be heard. First, Section 123 provides that tenants renting from a resident management council that acquired a project from a public housing authority "shall have all the rights provided to tenants of public housing," which presumably includes access to public housing lease and grievance procedures. In contrast, under PHHD, once a tenant buys his unit, he no longer has any continuing association with public housing. Further, under Section 123, HUD must offer all nonbuyers a housing voucher or Section 8 certificate as long as they continue to reside in the resident-owned project, even if the rent exceeds the established fair market rent. In the PHHD, this option is left up to the public housing authority. For nonbuying families who choose not to remain in their housing unit once their project is sold, HUD must provide, at the family's choice, either a comparable unit in another public housing project, or sufficient financial assistance to allow the family to move into a comparable private dwelling at no greater out-of-pocket cost. In either case, HUD is required to reimburse the family for relocation costs.

PHHD and Section 123 provisions differ considerably on the question of replacing sold housing stock. In PHHD, there are no formal public housing development funds to compensate public housing authorities for the loss of low-income housing stock. The rationale is that, since units sold must remain occupied by low-income families for five years (or longer if the public housing authority extends resale restrictions), the privatized housing will be part of the community's low-income housing supply for years to come.

The Section 123 homeownership initiative contains a one-for-one replacement requirement, which public housing authorities must implement within thirty months. Replacement units may come from "the production of new public housing units, the acquisition of existing units, the rehabilitation of vacant public housing units, or acquisition by the resident management corporation of non-publicly owned, decent, and affordable housing units, which the resident management corporation shall operate as rental housing subject to tenant income and rent limitations comparable to the limitations applicable to public housing."[40]

The Replacement-Housing Issue

There are no replacement-housing requirements associated with HUD's national Public Housing Homeownership Demonstration or any other Section 5(h) sales that transfer ownership of public housing units directly to tenants. But Congress did impose a one-for-one replacement-housing requirement on all Section 123 transfers of public housing projects to resident management councils.

Section 123 regulations require public housing authorities to replace all units sold to resident management councils within thirty months of sale.[41] Replacement may be made by constructing new public housing units, modernizing vacant public housing units, or allowing resident management councils to acquire and operate privately owned units as low-income rental housing.

At first, Congress provided HUD some "wiggle room" on the thirty-month time frame by not pinpointing when the clock began to tick. Then HUD decided that instead of requiring that replacement housing be ready for occupancy within thirty months, "the 30 month time period in the act refers to starting implementation of the replacement plan, not completion of the replacement units."[42] This had the effect of extending the time of putting replacement units in place to six years from the date that HUD transfers title to the resident management council.[43] Such an interpretation of intent seems to be far more generous than Congress intended.

It makes little sense to require replacement units under one privatization plan but not another. For one thing, it will inevitably affect the choice of legislative authority under which a public housing authority elects to design its privatization program. It would be far better if this decision were based on objectives, the extent of resident management in place, the characteristics of the public housing authority's inventory and waiting list, and so forth—not on whether the public housing authority can evade having to replace the units it sells.

To avoid the inevitable distortions that will arise because Section 123 and Section 5(h) sales treat replacement housing differently, the requirements under both legislative authorities should be the same.

However, reclaiming previously abandoned public housing units through modernization should not be considered replacement housing under any privatization program. In light of the national shortage of low-income housing, reclaiming vacant and derelict inventory for occupancy should be both HUD's and local public housing authorities' highest priority. Whether or not a public housing authority receives federal funds to accomplish this task should not depend on whether it is a participant in HUD's privatization efforts.

Rather than extend the replacement-housing requirement to Section 5(h) sales, HUD proposed, in 1989, liberalizing the Section 123 replacement-housing requirement by permitting public housing authorities to count as replacement units low-income housing constructed under state and locally funded programs. The administration now seems to be mounting a bold effort to repeal Section 123's replacement-housing provisions altogether.

According to a December 1989 report by the inspector general: "Section 21(a) (3) (c) [of the U.S. Housing Act of 1937] should be amended to eliminate the one-for-one replacement provision relating to project buy-outs by [resident management councils]. There simply are not enough housing development funds in HUD's budget to meet replacement housing needs under Section 21."[44] The report suggests that public housing authorities with privatization programs could wind up with a disproportionate share of modernization funds, compared to other public housing authorities in the allocation area that do not wish to sell off any of their stock.

Congress should deal with the inspector general's concerns by eliminating renovation of vacant public housing as a means of meeting the replacement-housing requirement. Further, the replacement-housing requirement itself should be adjusted. Instead of one-for-one replacement, the number of units that must be replaced should be reduced by the number of long-term vacancies that existed at the start of the buy-out process. (In other words, HUD should not have to bear the burden of replacing units that had been out of the active inventory for an extended period of time.)

Adoption of this proposal would reserve modernization funds for rebuilding public housing stock that will remain in public ownership, while still requiring HUD to replace all housing units slated for sale that are part of its active inventory. The fact that HUD has insufficient funds to meet either the existing Section 123 one-for-one replacement-housing requirement or the less restrictive requirement that I propose is a resource problem, not a flaw in the design of the public housing homeownership legislation.

New Initiatives

Resident management and resident sales are not the only, or even necessarily the most cost-effective, ways to deal with long-term dependence on public housing. Three recent initiatives designed to increase self-sufficiency and help families move out of public housing warrant mention because they are creative alternatives to resident management and privatization that seek to promote upward mobility—and, in some cases, homeownership—without having to sell off the public housing stock: the Lafayette Court Family Development Center in Baltimore and the Stepping Stone Housing and Gateway Housing programs in Charlotte, North Carolina. These initiatives are representative of a new genre of programs designed to restore public housing to its historical role as a temporary way station for families needing an inexpensive place to live while getting themselves together.

In Baltimore, almost half of all poor, black, single-parent households live in public housing, as do almost a tenth of all the city's children. Children comprise 40 percent of all public housing residents in Baltimore; their financial support comes through the welfare system. In 1986, almost half of all public housing residents in Baltimore received public assistance; for more than a third, this was their sole source of income.

The families who live in Lafayette Court, an 805-unit high-rise development containing 2,400 individuals—half of whom are children, and 85 percent of whom receive public assistance—are more representative of Baltimore's long-term public housing population than are the twenty-eight families who bought their homes under HUD's PHHD privatization program.[45]

In 1987, the city of Baltimore created the Lafayette Court Family Development Center to "alter the conditions that keep people poor and dependent on public assistance."[46] It is a multiagency effort coordinated by the public housing authority to reduce dependency and to strengthen the family unit through a coordinated program of education, health care, child care, counseling, and employment and training services. The package includes Head Start programs for infants and toddlers; on-site full day care for children; on-site computer-assisted learning labs; an on-site college degree program offered through Morgan State University; job counseling and job-search assistance; teen programs aimed at developing parenting and employment skills to promote self-sufficiency; and health screening, well-baby clinic services, and nutrition, family planning, and health-related education.

This is a collaborative effort of several local agencies. Lafayette Court's Advisory Board has representatives from the city's Office of Employment Development, Department of Housing and Community Development, the Health and Recreation departments, the Mayor's Office of Children and Youth, the city school system, and Lafayette Court's tenant council and resident advisory board.

Capital and some operating costs are budgeted from the city's Community Development Block Grant entitlement; employment and training services are funded from Job Training Partnership Act monies; and the city's Health and Recreation departments have provided both in-kind services and guidance in designing specifications for contracted services. Facilities and equipment for the preschool and the school-age children's program have been provided by the school system; day care has been funded by the state Department of Social Services.

Although formal evaluation of the Family Development Center is not yet complete—it is currently under evaluation by researchers from the Johns Hopkins University—its potential to support resident self-sufficiency was recognized by Congress in the 1990 National Affordable Housing Act, which authorized funds for up to five additional self-sufficiency demonstrations.

The Stepping Stone and Gateway Housing Programs administered by the Charlotte, North Carolina, public housing authority are complementary efforts also aimed at increasing self-sufficiency and helping families move out of public housing into homes of their own. Like Lafayette Court's Family Development Center, these programs are intended to reduce dependency by strengthening the family and increasing employment opportunities. They are more ambitious in that they seek to limit a family's stay in public housing to no more than five or seven years, respectively, thereby restoring public housing's original function of serving as a temporary haven for families in troubled times.

The Stepping Stone Housing Program, initiated in 1988, was designed to assist one hundred families living in public housing units. To participate, the families had to have stable employment and incomes of at least $12,500. Families applying for the Stepping Stone program agreed to move out of public housing into newly constructed apartments that were owned by the public housing authority but were not part of the public housing inventory. They agreed to pay a fixed rent for these apartments and "to terminate residency at the end of five years, if not sooner, and to seek residency on the private market."[47]

Families participating in the Stepping Stone program receive counseling on homeownership and are given opportunities for job training, continuing education, and skills development, as well as other services to enhance their earnings potential and job security. They must participate in a forced savings plan in association with their rental payments. Each year, their rent increases $15 a month; that additional rent must be put in an escrow account to be used later as a down payment on housing in the private market.

Also conceived in 1988, the Gateway Housing program is a more extensive, service-rich version of the Stepping Stone program for poorer, less self-sufficient families. It was designed to assist one hundred families living in public housing whose incomes were lower than those in the Stepping Stone program. To accomplish its goals, Gateway Housing contracts with families to deliver a customized mix of counseling and educational, health, and employment services. To encourage participation,

Gateway eliminates the punitive policies and regulations—such as raising the rent or dropping child-care benefits or health insurance as soon as an individual gets a job or works more hours—that are built into needs-based programs like Food Stamps, Aid to Families with Dependent Children, and public housing and that discourage families from wanting to better themselves and leave public housing.[48]

Families entering the Gateway Housing program are required to assess what it is that prevents them from reaching their goals and to make a commitment to overcome these impediments, with assistance, within a two-year time frame. For example, if the problem is lack of a high school degree or job-skills training, they agree to complete that degree or training within a two-year period. During that time, their rent will be frozen; if they are receiving public assistance, they will continue to receive it as long as they make progress in fulfilling their contract.

Once these barriers have been overcome, the family enters the second phase of the program, which cannot last more than five years. During this phase, their rent will increase in relationship to their income, as it normally would for residents of public housing. But a portion of their rent will be set aside in a savings account to be used as a down payment on a home or other private-market housing when they are ready to leave public housing. During this phase, families will receive assistance in upgrading their job skills, guidance on household accounting, homeownership, investments, and whatever else is deemed necessary to ensure the achievement of the participants' goals.[49]

At inception, approximately five hundred families requested information about the Gateway Housing program. But only sixty-four were prepared to meet the personal and family development goals that the two-year remediation phase of the program demands of them. As of this writing, recruitment efforts are continuing to fill the remaining places.

Because they fall outside of the resident management framework, neither the Lafayette Court Family Development Center nor the Stepping Stone or Gateway Housing programs have received any special funding from the Bush administration. But the fact that Congress explicitly recognized the potential of these public-housing-authority-sponsored self-sufficiency initiatives in its 1990 housing legislation suggests that the public housing reform pursued by Jack Kemp during his first two years at HUD—resident management followed by sale—will be considerably broadened in the years ahead. This is all to the good.

Chapter 5
FIVE CASE STUDIES

Thus far, the record on privatizing public housing has been mixed—especially with regard to multifamily units. As the following five case studies illustrate, neither so-called Section 5(h) sales, which require public housing residents to obtain immediate ownership interests in their apartments, nor so-called Section 123 transfers, in which the transition to homeownership occurs in two stages (title is transferred initially to a resident management council, which operates the property on a rental basis, then the project is converted to a limited equity co-op) are problem-free. While there are some promising privatization models, such as Louisville's College Court condominiums and Nashville's New Edition Co-op, the state of the art is still pretty crude.

Section 5(h) Sales to Tenants

Nashville's New Edition Co-op

Public housing authorities might learn from the New Edition Co-op model in Nashville, Tennessee, that in order to create a financially viable conversion using private financing, they may have to absorb a sizable portion of renovation costs.

As part of the PHHD demonstration, the Nashville, Tennessee, public housing authority used Community Development Block Grant funds to finance rehabilitation of an eighty-five-unit, scattered-site cooperative. The project, initiated in 1986, was completed and occupied in June 1989. To recover its $825,000 ($9,706/unit) capital investment in the rehabilitation, the public housing authority decided to sell the property to the co-op for the cost of the improvements. Financing plans projected $25,000 coming from initial co-op membership fees and $800,000 from a third-party, long-term mortgage loan—a loan that would be provided by the National Consumer Cooperative Bank.

The National Consumer Cooperative Bank's conservative underwriting and co-op preparedness standards, combined with its requirement for a market rate of return, made financing of this low-income conversion a safe and attractive investment for the bank. The public housing authority believed that the New Edition's property appraisal of $1,825,000 provided sufficient protection to secure an $800,000 loan (which would result in a loan-to-value ratio of less than 45 percent). The public housing authority was wrong.

By the time that the National Consumer Cooperative Bank signed off on the co-op's pro forma operating budget, confident that current operating costs and future replacement requirements were not being underestimated, the lender had significantly reduced the amount of cash flow available for debt service.

The bank added a 5 percent vacancy loss allowance and another 5 percent operating and replacement reserve requirement that had to be met out of current income. In addition, the bank used a conservative debt coverage ratio of 1.15, which meant that the co-op's projected income available for debt service had to equal 115 percent of actual mortgage payments. As a result, the bank approved a first mortgage loan of just $550,000. The $250,000 difference between the $825,000 cost and the sum of the loan plus co-op membership fees ($575,000) had to be absorbed by the public housing authority.

Another problem may result from future increases in interest rates. The bank's loan to New Edition is for fifteen years at a variable-rate interest starting at 11.875 percent. Interest rate adjustments will be made at the end of the fifth and tenth years, based on the average rate of five-year treasuries plus 3 percent. Whether these interest rate adjustments will result in a reduction or increase in the co-op's future debt-service burden is unknown. But the mere fact that the mortgage is subject to upward interest rate adjustments, which are independent of changes in the co-op members' ability to pay, adds a measure of uncertainty to the co-op's future.

There are two lessons that other public housing authorities can learn from the New Edition conversion. One is that the National Consumer Cooperative Bank is a willing lender—albeit one that demands market-rate returns and as much protection against risk of loss as any other private lending institution. The other is that public housing authorities must be prepared to absorb the portion of renovation costs that cannot be supported by monthly carrying charges.

Denver's Arapahoe Co-op

Like Nashville's New Edition Co-op, the rehabilitation of Denver's forty-four-unit Arapahoe co-op was accomplished (in 1988) without using any of the public housing authority's allocation of HUD modernization funds (needed to renovate deteriorated public housing projects remaining in rental occupancy). What is unique about Arapahoe is that it is the first public housing homeownership conversion in the country that was structured as a rental co-op in order to take advantage of federal low-income housing tax credits. As will be seen, this proved to be both a strength and a weakness.

Structuring the conversion as a rental co-op rather than a more traditional owner co-op enabled the public housing authority to syndicate, or sell to a private investor, the federal income tax credits generated by rehabilitation of the housing. In the process, the Denver Housing Authority earned $1,350,000 in gross syndication proceeds, and netted more than $1 million on the transaction. The net proceeds will be used by the Denver Housing Authority to acquire additional low-income housing stock.

Under the low-income housing tax credit provisions of the 1986 Tax Reform Act, all rehabilitated projects must remain low-income rental properties for at least fifteen years. Therefore, the Denver Housing Authority could not transfer title of the Arapahoe buildings to the cooperative corporation itself. But what the public housing authority could do was to transfer title to a third party—a limited partnership specifically formed for the purpose—in exchange for purchase of the project's federal income tax credits; the limited partnership could then lease the housing units to the co-op for the requisite fifteen years, at which time it could sell the buildings to the co-op for a nominal price.

The centerpiece of the Arapahoe conversion is the Arapahoe Redevelopment Partnership, Ltd., a limited partnership consisting of three partners. The general partner is the Arapahoe Cooperative Corporation, whose shareholders are the forty-four public housing tenants who want to become homeowners. The limited partner is a wealthy private investor (a local Denver corporation) that acquired the federal income tax credits associated with the redevelopment of Arapahoe for the sum of $1,350,000.

After the co-op and the limited partnership were formed, the Denver Housing Authority sold the buildings and other facilities to the partnership in exchange for $1,350,000 cash, which was the approximate cost of redeveloping the Arapahoe project, and a promissory note in the amount of $1,650,000. The note has a fixed interest rate of 5.25 percent and carries a twenty-five-year term. The transfer provided that the buildings be used for low-income housing for an indefinite period.

Prior to transferring title to the buildings to the partnership, the Denver Housing Authority transferred title to the project's land to the co-op for the price of one dollar—subject to a twenty-five-year ground lease. The partnership must pay a ground rent of one dollar a year for the first fifteen years of the lease. If the partnership continues to lease the ground for the last ten years of the lease, it must pay the ground's full rental value for each of those years. Increasing the ground rent to market value after fifteen years, which is when the holding period for the tax credits expires, is intended to force the partnership to sell the buildings to the cooperative. At this point, the cooperative would own the land and buildings subject to the public housing authority's outstanding first mortgage. In this way, the buildings would remain low-income housing for an indefinite period. Even without the sale, title to the improvements would revert to the cooperative when the ground lease expires.

The cooperative has an exclusive option to purchase the buildings after fifteen years at the greater of the market value of the property or the outstanding value of the public housing authority's mortgage (which will be approximately $922,000). Since the combined effects of the ground-lease restrictions and the continuing-use restrictions on the buildings will depress their market value, the public housing authority believes that the co-op is virtually guaranteed the right to acquire the buildings at the mortgage value. Since the co-op's rent to the partnership was set at the level needed to service the mortgage it will assume when it buys the buildings, the Denver Housing Authority is confident that the option to purchase is economically sound.

As part of its efforts to maximize the equity investment and to provide the limited partner with a competitive rate of return, the public housing authority felt it had to give absolute assurance that it could sell its interests in the partnership at the end of fifteen years at a price both known at the time of the initial closing and sufficient to pay the limited partner's federal tax liability due upon sale. This was accomplished by giving the limited partner a "put" option, exercisable at the end of fifteen years, to transfer its partnership interest to the public housing authority at a known price. The price was negotiated to be $691,000.

But agreeing on a price and assuring the limited partner that the public housing authority would have the necessary funds available to satisfy the put option are two different things. The way this problem was resolved was that the public housing authority acquired a sufficient quantity of deep-discount zero-coupon U.S. treasury bonds having fifteen-year maturities to accumulate to a value of $691,000 in the year 2003. At the time of closing, T-bill interest rates were around 9 percent. It was a simple matter for the public housing authority to determine that it needed to acquire $167,500 in face value of the bonds in order to accumulate $691,000 in fifteen years. The public housing authority used a portion of the limited partner's $1.35 million in equity contributions to pay for the bonds, as well as to underwrite all other costs of syndicating the tax credits.

Under the resale scenario, the limited partner is certain to exercise its put option at the end of fifteen years, at which time the public housing authority will transfer ownership of the buildings to the co-op at a price equal to the outstanding value of the mortgage. With just ten years remaining on the public housing authority's note, the co-op will own all land and buildings associated with the Arapahoe Cooperative free and clear, at the end of twenty-five years.

HUD has properly raised serious questions about the project and whether the conversion satisfies the requirements of Section 5(h), the legislative authority under which the national Public Housing Homeownership Demonstration was carried out. According to HUD, a Section 5(h) sale must "vest the tenants with rights incident to ownership, such as possession and control of the project (both land and improvements) upon conveyance [and] we cannot see such evidence of ownership in [this sale]."[1]

HUD also has voiced concern that Arapahoe tenants were not involved in the formative stages of the conversion, as required under PHHD guidelines. HUD believes that participants might have been misled into thinking that they were buying into a limited equity co-op when, in fact, they would be renters for a minimum of fifteen years. HUD also is concerned that the public housing authority and the limited partner have the potential to exercise excessive control over the co-op. The agency also questioned whether the co-op's option-to-purchase clause in the lease agreement is too conditional to assure conveyance at the end of the fifteen-year lease term. Finally, HUD questions whether the co-op will be able to afford to buy the project at the end of the lease term.

In addition to HUD's quite proper technical and legal concerns, the Arapahoe conversion raises other important questions, not the least of which is whether the hypothesized behavioral impacts of homeownership will occur when a group of low-income families control but do not own the cooperative housing they occupy. Moreover, because individual shareholder payments to the co-op are passed along to the partnership as rent payments under the co-op's long-term lease, neither the co-op nor individual Arapahoe shareholders can establish their respective institutional and individual credit records by systematically paying off their mortgage debt.

Louisville's College Court Condominiums

One of the most successful privatization efforts in the country is College Court, a public housing project that was converted to home-ownership by the Housing Authority of Louisville in 1988. Although the conversion of College Court was not part of HUD's homeownership demonstration, it was accomplished with HUD approval under the same statutory authority as the PHHD.

College Court is one of the oldest public housing projects in the country, built in 1938 by the Works Progress Administration. It is com-posed mostly of garden apartments, and features pillared balconies and porches, arches and covered walkways, and common courtyards. The complex is located directly south of Louisville's central business district in the heart of the city's designated Enterprise Zone, where intensive economic development is taking place. Because of its good location, well-landscaped, pedestrian-oriented style, and attractive architectural design, College Court was a natural selection for the public housing author-ity's first privatization initiative. Converting the complex to tenant ownership would preserve this unique housing resource and help fill the void in Louisville's low-income housing sales market. Further, the public housing authority would leverage the income generated from the sale of College Court units to create additional affordable owner-occupied housing for public housing residents and open up more conventional public housing rental units to families on the waiting list.

At the start of the conversion, the mayor pledged that College Court tenants who wished to acquire units and were financially able to do so would receive first priority. Also, any tenants who did not qualify or were not interested in buying could, with the help of housing vouchers, remain at College Court as renters.

Because nearly two-thirds of College Court's 126 units were effi-ciencies and one-bedroom apartments, while only 8 percent of eligi-ble applicants were waiting for such small units, the complex had to be not only rehabilitated but also reconfigured. The $3.2 million total renovation of the College Court complex began in mid-1986. The new College Court Condominiums consist of one hundred units, 94 percent of which have two or three bedrooms. The renovations included new roofs and landscaping, as well as the installation of new plumbing sys-tems and modern kitchens. The Housing Authority of Louisville delayed such finish work as interior painting, carpeting, and floor tiling until sales agreements were executed so that the units could be customized to the tastes of the new homeowners.

Pricing. When the rehabilitation was complete, College Court condominiums were appraised at between $21,000 and $22,000. Using conventional mortgage underwriting ratios, the public housing authority determined that prospective buyers could afford prices in the $12,000–$13,000 range, and set prices from a low of $8,700 for the six one-bedroom units to a high of $13,700 for the nineteen three-bedroom units. Depending on their configuration, the seventy-five two-bedroom units were priced from $11,000 to $11,700.

The difference between the appraised value and the discounted price represents the equity the buyer receives upon purchase of a College Court Condominium. Although College Court Condominiums are fully taxable by the city, which sets tax value at the sales price, it is the subsidized price at which the buyer's taxes are fixed—not the appraised value. This practice of setting tax value at the subsidized, rather than the market, value could be especially critical in high-tax, high-subsidy jurisdictions like Washington, D.C., where the average price paid for a public housing condo conversion was $35,000 less than its appraised value.[2]

Several months into the sales period, public housing authority officials concluded they had underpriced all College Court units—especially the larger ones. The prices were increased to $11,000–$12,000 for a one-bedroom unit; $14,000–$18,500 for a two-bedroom unit (depending on location, features, and whether or not the unit had an extra half-bath); and $20,000–$23,000 for a three-bedroom unit. Despite the higher prices, all condominiums have been sold—save for nine units rented by original College Court tenants—and there is a substantial waiting list for units that might become available for resale.

Financing. Renovation and rehabilitation was financed approximately two-thirds by HUD modernization funds ($2 million) and one-third by state and local funds. The public housing authority contributed $800,000 from its own reserve funds; the city of Louisville contributed $214,000 in Community Development Block Grant funds; and the final $170,000 came from the state of Kentucky Energy Conservation Bank.

Mortgage payments on the College Court condominiums range from a low of $67 to a high of $106. Condominium fees—which include charges for water, fire insurance, and what public housing authority officials call a 100 percent replacement reserve that covers the full replacement of all major capital systems—range from $67 to $126 a month. Thus the total monthly costs of these condominiums ranges from $127 to $230. Based on the price, financing terms, and common-area expenses, the minimum monthly income needed to qualify for a College Court condominium was $800. Most buyers have annual incomes of $12,000–$13,000, which is enough to qualify.

In qualifying buyers for initial purchase, the public housing authority uncovered a serious problem: unreported income among College Court public housing tenants. HUD officials raised the subject of tenant fraud at a March 1987 meeting with the public housing authority staff, stressing their concern that residents who had defrauded the public housing authority in the past—by not reporting income during periodic income recertifications—should not be permitted to buy their units. To qualify as homebuyers, approximately one-third of the applicants for College Court units divulged income that they had not previously reported to the public housing authority for purposes of recomputing rental rates. All thirty-one families were disqualified from the program, and new applicants were recruited in their place.

The public housing authority financed the sale of College Court condominiums through a 5 percent, twenty-five-year mortgage. But it does not service College Court loans. Loan servicing is done by Louisville Housing Services, a nonprofit subsidiary of the housing authority, for the fee of three dollars per unit per month. This arrangement encourages buyer independence, enables Louisville Housing Services to employ "market-oriented" servicing policies that promote full and timely loan payments, and makes it unnecessary for the public housing authority to report these loan payments as income to HUD, which would otherwise have reduced its operating subsidies.

In order to secure full and timely loan payments, Louisville Housing Services decided that it would not accept mortgage payments without full payment of condominium fees. (When it did allow split payment, delinquencies on condominium fees ran quite high.) A $15 late fee is assessed if payment in full is not received by the fifteenth of the month; late payments that are not accompanied by the late fee are not accepted.

If a family cannot keep up with its financial obligation, the public housing authority will buy back the unit at its original cost (discounting the price for any buyer-caused damages). While the public housing authority will rebuy any unit any time during the twenty-five-year life of the loan, it will not give the family any equity. Thus far, two years after the initial sales, the public housing authority has not had to take back any units, and most buyers have established excellent payment records, although five families (6 percent of all buyers) have been persistently late in making their payments.

Resale Restrictions. Resale restrictions on College Court condominiums are rather liberal. Because the public housing authority estimates that the original condominium prices were about $9,000 below market value, families that choose to sell their units within six years of purchase must pay back some or all of that initial discount. If a unit is resold within two years, the initial owner must pay both the outstanding mortgage balance and the full $9,000. Recapture of the initial discount falls to $6,000 for a resale between three and five years after purchase; and to $3,000 in year six. After six years, there is no recapture or other restrictions on resale.

Counseling. Because the public housing authority's counselors believe that preparing low-income families for their initial home purchase is essential to program success, all buyers were required to attend individual and group counseling sessions. These prepurchase sessions, conducted by an independent consultant who helped design and implement the conversion and manage the College Court Condominiums, covered such topics as mortgage finance, the legal structure of a condominium, the tax benefits of homeownership, and home maintenance. But much of what takes place in formal classroom sessions may need to be reiterated on a one-to-one basis after closing, when families have moved into their homes and are on their own—especially instruction in money management and home maintenance.

Program officials in Louisville believe that it takes three to five years for a low-income public housing tenant who has been a renter all her life to make a complete transition—which includes taking full responsibility for unit maintenance—to homeownership. Part of the transition is acquisition of basic home-maintenance skills; part is adjusting to the reality that when something goes wrong with the house, the buyer cannot blame the landlord, wait for him to fix it, or ignore the problem because "it's not my property anyway." Although the Housing Authority of Louisville did not set up a formal postpurchase counseling program for College Court buyers, the management company, whose contractual obligations did not include interior unit repairs, decided to instruct owners in basic home maintenance on the grounds that improving resident care of the property would improve overall property management. Thus, the manager showed families how to do such preventive maintenance on their units as changing furnace filters and fixing toilet leaks. When the management company carried out a repair, the owner was instructed on how the repair is done, with the understanding that the next time, the owner will take care of the problem. If the same problem recurs and the owner calls management to fix it, the owner is charged for the service.

Selling Public Housing to Create More Housing. Louisville's conversion of College Court was authorized under Section 5(h) of the National Housing Act, and, as such, the public housing authority was not obligated to replace any of the sold units. Nonetheless, the housing authority devised a way to leverage the income generated from the sale of College Court to develop and finance thirty-six new condominium units for sale to public housing residents.

Unlike the sale of tax credits associated with the rehabilitation of the Arapahoe co-op, which earned the Denver public housing authority more than $1 million in cash, the sale of College Court condominiums generated little upfront cash. This is because the Louisville public housing authority provided no-down-payment, 100 percent loans to College Court buyers. Still, the public housing authority has some cash flow coming in from College Court. After accounting for all property management costs, the College Court Condominiums generate about $8,000 a month, which comes from the buyer's mortgage payments and rental receipts from the nine families that continue to occupy their College Court units as renters (with Section 8 assistance).

The three sites for the thirty-six new condominium units were donated, for the most part, by the city and are located in marginal neighborhoods. In addition, the public housing authority purchased a few inexpensive, contiguous lots adjacent to one site. Although it was important to achieve a high presale rate to ensure that occupants would move in when construction was completed (to achieve the critical mass of homeowners necessary to create a sense of neighborhood), the developer did not build a model unit—a standard marketing tool—because of fear of vandalism. Instead, the public housing authority marketed the condominiums by publicizing the overwhelming success of the College Court project. Thirty-one of the thirty-six units were presold.

The two- and three-bedroom condominiums were developed by the Louisville Housing Development Corporation, a local nonprofit organization that packages financing for low- and moderate-income housing. Each unit has central air conditioning, a heat pump, wall-to-wall carpeting, a self-cleaning oven, and a frost-free refrigerator. Because the condominiums were sold at cost—$31,950 for a two-bedroom unit, $36,000 for a three-bedroom unit (which approximates their market value)—the public housing authority did not impose resale restrictions.

Financing was provided through a public/private partnership between the city, Liberty National Bank, and Louisville Housing Services (the nonprofit subsidiary of the public housing authority that serviced loans for the College Court condominiums).

Liberty National Bank provided Louisville Housing Services with a 7 percent, thirty-year loan for the entire cost of the project. These generous terms were the result of Liberty National's efforts to improve its rating under the Federal Community Reinvestment Act, which requires lenders to meet the credit needs of their local communities. The bank loan was secured by a 7 percent, thirty-year second mortgage from the Louisville Housing Development Corporation for 25 percent of total development costs (guaranteed by the city), and by assignment of the College Court mortgages to Liberty National Bank. Another condition of Liberty National's participation was that the company that managed the College Court condominiums manage the new development.

Louisville Housing Services provided no-down-payment, 100 percent loans to individual buyers at a 10.5 percent interest rate for thirty years. (Buyers had to contribute $500 in cash, though, to help offset closing costs.) When a buyer closed, documents were filed for the unit purchased, and Liberty National released an individual mortgage.

After aggregating the mortgage payments from all individual buyers, Louisville Housing Services makes one monthly payment to Liberty National and one to the city. This way, according to program officials, it would take a catastrophic default rate—in the neighborhood of 30–40 percent—to threaten the security of the bank loan. Even if default on such a large scale were to happen, Louisville Housing Services is authorized to suspend payments on the city's loan to make good on the private loan. Louisville Housing Services also can use cash from College Court mortgage payments to help meet a temporary cash deficit.

Monthly carrying charges average $302 for a two-bedroom unit and $340 for a three-bedroom unit. This includes full debt services; taxes; insurance; a fee for common electrical, water, and sewer service; all exterior and some interior maintenance; management costs; and a 100 percent capital replacement reserve.

Using the income generated from the College Court conversion and the point spread between its lower cost of money (7 percent) and the higher interest rate it charged to buyers (10.5 percent), Louisville Housing Services has been able to subsidize each buyer's carrying charges by approximately $70 a month—which is more than 20 percent. This subsidy enables public housing residents with incomes between $13,000 and $14,000 to become homeowners.

Not all public housing authorities will be able to replicate the Housing Authority of Louisville's success in leveraging income generated from privatizing public housing to create additional affordable homeownership opportunities. For one thing, construction costs in Louisville are much lower than they are in many other communities, where additional federal subsidies may be necessary. For another, in too many communities, nonprofit development entities compete with the local housing authority for scarce development funds, instead of working with the local housing authority to develop cost-effective housing. This, however, does not have to be.

The Louisville case study demonstrates that privatization can be a strategic tool in a public housing authority's arsenal—enabling it to extend the useful life of older developments and to provide homeownership opportunities for upwardly mobile, working families that live in public housing rental units, where rules penalize ambition and the work ethic. It also demonstrates that expanding homeownership opportunities frees up rental housing units for very poor families waiting for apartments. This benefit, though, can only materialize if more owner units are created than rental units are removed from the inventory. In Louisville's case, the reconfiguration and privatization of College Court and the subsequent development of thirty-six new condominiums resulted in a net increase of ten affordable units in the city.

Section 123 Transfers to Resident Management Councils

Section 123 transfers are initiated when a resident management council buys its development from the public housing authority—an act that permanently removes the housing from public ownership and from continued eligibility for long-term operating assistance. This acquisition privatizes the public housing project but does not alter the rental status—or improve the rent-paying abilities—of the residents, who now become tenants of the resident management council. It is only when the resident management council converts the housing project to a limited equity cooperative or condominium that resident ownership is actually accomplished.

At the beginning of the Bush administration, only thirteen resident management councils had active contracts to manage public housing properties—and not all of these were either qualified or interested in buying their projects.[3] Within the past two years, HUD has provided funds to enrich the programs of existing resident management councils and to create up to seventy more.

Currently, just two resident management councils—Kenilworth-Parkside in Washington, D.C., and Carr Square Village in St. Louis—have sought HUD approval to acquire their projects. But with the enactment of the administration's HOPE privatization initiatives as part of the National Affordable Housing Act in October 1990 (authorizing substantial funding for homeownership programs), the public housing sales pipeline is likely to grow.

Washington, D.C.'s Kenilworth-Parkside

Built in 1959, the 464-unit Kenilworth-Parkside project is currently undergoing major renovations that have thus far cost the government more than $25 million ($54,241 per unit).[4] Transfer of ownership to the resident management council occurred on September 28, 1990, and the project is slated for conversion to resident ownership five years from then.

But whether projections call for Kenilworth-Parkside to be held as a rental project for five or fifteen years (or something in between), given the low incomes of its residents, the resident management council simply will not be able to survive unless it is able to replace the lost operating subsidies.

Plans for interim support have been announced. According to the General Accounting Office, "HUD plans to assist Kenilworth-Parkside financially with Section 8 project-based rental certificates and vouchers ... limited to the amount of operating subsidy HUD estimates it would have provided during the period had Kenilworth-Parkside remained public housing." A technical consultant to Kenilworth-Parkside estimates this assistance will add up to roughly $1.8 million per year ($362 per unit per month).[5]

It is reasonable to presume that in enacting the resident ownership program, Congress did not intend to create a new low-income rental program that would save HUD some public housing operating subsidies while draining scarce rental assistance funds that otherwise would be used to help inadequately housed low-income families to find suitable shelter.

In the early stages of the Kenilworth-Parkside conversion, HUD's position was that these subsidies to resident-owners during the process of transition would not be long term. Later on, under the HOPE legislation, the concept of interim assistance came to mean more than five years of operating support, starting from the time the project is transferred to the resident management council. In response to the inspector general's suggestion that "housing ownership by low-income families may not be feasible without the use of significant subsidy mechanisms," HUD responded that "this view has been disproved by the ... homeownership sales demonstration. Four multi-family sales to low-income cooperatives or condo associations in Washington, D.C., Denver, Nashville, and Paterson requiring no after-sale subsidies, provide positive examples."[6]

But HUD is not entirely forthcoming on this matter. For one thing, the Paterson closing never took place. First, because too few tenants decided to join the co-op to make it financially viable; second, because litigation over public housing authority pressures to move nonbuyers into other public housing projects brought the conversion to a halt. Although not mentioned by HUD, another planned conversion in St. Thomas, Virgin Islands, never closed because of low tenant incomes and problems with relocating nonbuyers.[7] Also, the Denver public housing authority, which is experiencing continued high vacancy rates and payment delinquencies at its Upper Lawrence co-op, may resort to using a portion of its Section 8 rental assistance allocation to subsidizing the project.[8]

The preliminary financing plan for Kenilworth-Parkside's conversion was based on the premise that, once the project was completely rehabilitated at government expense and transferred to the resident management council for a dollar, the new homeowners would be sufficiently roused by the empowerment experience to increase their incomes and earn their way off subsidy in relatively short order. At the heart of the financing plan was an operating reserve account to make up the difference between resident payments and the actual costs of running the co-op. The reserve fund would be largely capitalized from surplus cash generated by the Section 8 rental assistance that the project is receiving from HUD during the interim period in which it is owned by the resident management corporation. The combination of anticipated increases in resident incomes (due to economic development activities by the resident management council) and internally generated subsidies from the operating reserve will, according to the project's planners, keep the co-op affordable and operating in the black over the long term.

Not so, according to the General Accounting Office, which claims that "(1) the long-term success of Kenilworth-Parkside appears contingent upon the ability to raise tenant incomes by 6 percent annually and (2) the supply of funds from within Kenilworth-Parkside's budget to support the education and services to realize this increase appears questionable." The General Accounting Office believes instead that "the project could not support itself beyond year 13."[9]

In response, one of Kenilworth-Parkside's financial consultants lamely defended the assumption of a 6 percent annual increase in the incomes of Kenilworth-Parkside owners over the long term, stating: "In order to prove themselves financially capable of purchasing their apartments, a significant number of families will declare the additional income they are already making."[10]

He is probably right about the unreported income, but this has to do with fraudulent behavior, not with the empowering effects of home-ownership. As discussed earlier, public housing authority officials in Louisville, Kentucky, found a very high rate of unreported incomes among College Court tenants who wanted to buy their apartments. The potentially high rate of underreported incomes among resident-owners should be kept in mind when evaluating how effective resident-management-council-operated educational, employment, and entrepreneurial development programs are in increasing incomes.

Rather than having to put its inadequate financial plan into effect, Congress resolved Kenilworth-Parkside's short-term cash flow problems by authorizing HUD to continue subsidizing rental operations of privatized public housing projects from the time they are acquired by a resident management council until they are converted to owner occupancy. During this period, assistance for operating expenses is limited to the amount the project would have received had it remained part of the public housing stock. However, by limiting postconversion operating assistance to just five years, Congress bought into the untested proposition that this left enough time for the benefits of job training and other economic development initiatives that were designed into Kenilworth-Parkside's privatization plans to pay off. Whether resident incomes will flow rapidly enough to enable them to pay their own way when the operating subsidies end remains questionable.

Just as it failed to deal with the interim cash flow deficit in resident-council-owned rental projects, which the HOPE legislation subsequently corrected, so, too, did Section 123 ignore the issue of how the costly improvements to these properties should be financed. There is no separate appropriation of "modernization funds" for projects slated for sale to resident management councils. Therefore, every public housing project that remains in public ownership is in competition for every dollar of capital subsidy to a property that will be privatized. On the surface, at least, HOPE partially resolved this problem by creating a separate pool of funds to pay for the renovation of public housing projects slated for privatization. However, the administration's fiscal year 1992 budget proposes to fund the HOPE program in part by using unspent 1991 appropriations that Congress targeted for the construction of new public housing. Moreover, while the public housing modernization program contains no local matching requirement, the HOPE legislation requires a substantial (25 percent) local match. Given the extreme shortage of low-income housing, it is hard to imagine why a community would choose the option of underwriting a quarter of the cost of privatizing a public housing project over the alternative of using its scarce resources to expand the local supply of low-rent and affordable housing.

Whether it remains publicly owned for years to come or is slated for sale to residents, the cost of renovating older public housing is not cheap. But the costlier it is, the less sense it makes for the government to underwrite the necessary improvements and then give the project away for nothing. Modernization costs for public housing are notoriously high in the District of Columbia, largely because the stock is in such poor condition and the local public housing authority has been poorly managed for a long time. Still, on a per unit basis, the anticipated cost to HUD of modernizing Kenilworth-Parkside ($73,806+) is 138 percent higher than the district average ($31,000); 409 percent higher than the average across the HUD region of which the District of Columbia is part ($14,500); and 738 percent greater than the national average ($10,000).[11]

Even if renovation costs exceed market value by a wide margin, if not prohibited from doing so through deed restrictions or legislation, a resident management council could use its property as collateral for mortgage loans to finance additional facilities and amenities, which would raise the purchase price to low-income buyers. In fact, Kenilworth-Parkside's original posttransfer improvement plans called for the installation of a year-round ". . . swimming pool, a licensed kitchen to prepare residents for careers in the food preparation industry, tennis courts, racquetball courts, and ceiling fans plus two window air conditioning units per apartment."[12]

The General Accounting Office correctly recognized that "a loan taken out to finance these items would increase the operating costs for the property and could delay the conversion to tenant ownership because each tenant would need increased income to support his or her share of the operating costs."[13] It therefore urged HUD to regulate Kenilworth-Parkside as well as other resident management council borrowing activities. In response, HUD's Office of Resident Initiatives adopted a regulation that would "require HUD approval of any loan taken out by a RMC using the property as collateral" in an effort to "protect the residents against financial mismanagement by a RMC."[14] This regulation was later embodied into law as part of the HOPE legislation.

Section 123 is silent on how long a resident management council may own a housing project before converting it to resident ownership. Kenilworth-Parkside expects a conversion in 1995, but these plans are not firm. The General Accounting Office took HUD to task for approving transfer of ownership to the resident management council without explicit plans for achieving resident ownership. According to the General Accounting Office, HUD's 1988 plan for privatizing Kenilworth-Parkside "focused almost exclusively on transferring ownership to the RMC. Likewise, additional technical planning initiated subsequently by consultants focused almost exclusively on the feasibility of an ownership transfer to the RMC. Neither of these efforts addressed items such as the price of ownership shares that tenants can afford, nor how the tenants will finance them."[15]

As a result of the Kenilworth-Parkside experience, the General Accounting Office recommended that HUD assess the feasibility of tenant ownership before title to a public housing property is transferred to its resident management council. Draft legislation prepared by the Senate Housing Subcommittee staff went even further, recommending that a new section be added to the public housing homeownership statute to specifically prohibit HUD from transferring title to a resident management council before ensuring that:

> The resident management corporation has a workable plan for giving all tenants an opportunity to become owners, which plan shall identify
> (I) the price at which the corporation intends to sell individual units or cooperative shares in the project;
> (II) the factors that will influence the setting of such price;
> (III) how such price compares to the estimated appraised value of the units or shares;
> (IV) the underwriting standards the corporation plans to use for potential tenant purchasers;
> (V) the financing arrangements the tenants are expected to pursue or be provided;
> (VI) a workable schedule of sale based on estimated tenant incomes; and
> (VII) the resident management corporation has certified that it will transfer ownership of the property to tenants within a specified period of time that the Secretary determines to be reasonable.[16]

With many of the staff's planning recommendations now incorporated into the HOPE legislation, the pace of public housing homeownership efforts will inevitably slow, since housing authorities and privatization ideologues can no longer "wing it." This is good because the costs of poor planning, unrealistic budgeting, and exaggerated expectations will be borne by the families that the privatization programs are intended to serve. No legislation enacted to date provides for the return to public ownership of partially privatized projects or converted co-ops that cannot meet their financial obligations.

Carr Square Village

Built in 1942, Carr Square contains 658 units and requires, according to preliminary estimates, more than $32 million in rehabilitation. Preliminary plans for the sale of Carr Square Village call for a resident management council to maintain the project in rental use for fifteen years, at the end of which time it would be converted to resident ownership.

The resident management council's initial application to HUD proposed a tax credit transaction similar to the Arapahoe project: HUD would transfer the buildings to a limited partnership made up of a corporate general partner and individual limited partners. The resident management council would play a controlling role in managing the property and would have the right to purchase the buildings from the partnership when the partnership expired (after fifteen years) at a reasonable price.[17]

This Arapahoe-type sale and conversion—which violated the spirit and intent of Section 5(h)—is permitted under Section 123, which does not require direct sale to individual resident-buyers. Some public housing authorities and resident management councils might find the rental approach to privatization desirable for the following reasons. First, private capital is used to help finance rehabilitation (avoiding exclusive reliance on scarce public housing modernization funds that should be used to renovate projects that will remain in public ownership). Under HOPE, reducing the federal contribution to renovation costs also reduces the required local match. Second, although the administration sees homeownership as the logical end result of a successful resident management experience, not all resident management organizations have the same vision. While many tenants in resident-managed projects want a home of their own, this does not necessarily mean that they want to buy their public housing unit.

When asked why a long-term rental arrangement was chosen over an ownership-type conversion, an individual close to the Carr Square buy-out explained that "but for Section 123, Carr Square will not get renovated and turned into a community that provides decent, safe and sanitary housing. It will just continue to deteriorate. . . . I see privatization as a way of generating cash for renovation and preservation of real estate and the community over the long run."

Basically, he said, "we have no interest in co-op conversion. . . . The objective of the Carr Square redevelopment is the creation of a financially-viable, economically-integrated rental housing development that would improve the living conditions of current residents, discourage those with the resources to do so from leaving and attracting back to the complex successful families who moved out as conditions deteriorated. . . .

"The tax credit," he continued, "provides a mechanism to intervene in the cycle of decay—a way of rehabilitating the property and creating a source of on-going subsidy to maintain its low income character. It gives the project a 15 year period in which to establish its economic strength and stability and be reintroduced into the community as something other than a stigmatized public housing project."

Given the shortage of federal funds and the fact that HUD modernization monies cannot be used to finance many amenities necessary for modern living, it is urgent to involve the corporate sector, through the use of tax credits, in the redevelopment of seriously deteriorated public housing developments. The fact is that a Carr Square buy-out is highly replicable as a straight tax credit rental project where tenants can be trained to take over ownership at the end of fifteen years. It is a realistic model for recycling hundreds of derelict public housing projects.

The plan submitted to HUD in July 1989 proposed that no public housing modernization funds be used in the reconstruction of Carr Square. Instead, the $32.1 million cost would be covered through a combination of mortgage loans, grants, and equity investments from the public and private sectors. More than a third of the cost ($11.5 million) would be covered by equity raised through the sale of tax credits to private investors. Slightly less than half the resources ($15.6 million) would come from long-term loans from the state housing finance agency, and the remaining $5 million from a grant from the city of St. Louis.

Under federal law, a project that uses tax credits must reserve either 20 percent of its units for families with incomes at or below 50 percent of the local median or 40 percent of the units for families with incomes no higher than 60 percent of the median. Initial plans for Carr Square called for 75 percent of the units to be reserved for families at or below 60 percent of the median level; the remaining 25 percent would be available to families earning up to 80 percent of median income.

Without rental assistance, the typical Carr Square resident—whose income averages just $7,000 a year—would be unable to pay the

$410-a-month rent needed to meet the project's full debt-service and operating requirements. This is where Carr Square's internal operating- subsidy fund and HUD Section 8 rental assistance come into the picture.

The internal subsidy was to be generated from interest earned on an operating reserve fund capitalized at the time of initial title transfer (using $2.6 million of the city's $5 million grant). The Section 8 assistance, which would have an average initial value of $296 a month, would be in the form of five- and fifteen-year project-based rental certificates attached to each of Carr Square's 485 rental units. How quickly the rental assistance could be phased out would depend on the income mix at the start of operations, the rate at which resident incomes increased over time relative to project expenses, and changes in the tenant mix.

(It should be kept in mind that a high proportion of Carr Square Village tenants are elderly, and that their incomes and rent-paying abilities are lower, for example, than those of Kenilworth-Parkside residents. Also, because Carr Square tenants are elderly, their rate of income growth will be lower than that of Kenilworth-Parkside residents—especially if the latter's job training programs succeed in upgrading residents' employment skills.)

When reviewing the plans for privatizing Carr Square, HUD's inspector general raised questions about whether allocating more than 400 housing vouchers to the residents of Carr Square would deprive other public housing authorities in the region of "their normal fair share of Section 8 assistance."[18] HUD advised the inspector general that "there is no anticipated impact from the Carr Square purchase on the level of Section 8 assistance that will be available for other PHAs in Region VII since the Section 8 assistance is proposed to come from a '*Headquarters allocation.*'"[19] [emphasis added] The inspector general found HUD's response somewhat disingenuous, stating that "the Secretary recently announced his intention to eliminate Headquarters discretionary reserve funding. Therefore, we are not certain where this Headquarters allocation will come from."[20]

The Senate Subcommittee on Housing has taken the view that the allocation of project-based rental assistance to tenant-owned public housing projects would unfairly penalize families waiting for housing assistance. Under legislation introduced in November 1989, the subcommittee proposed prohibiting such aid to resident-owned projects. The HOPE (privatization) measure enacted by Congress in October 1990 does ban such aid, while permitting HUD to continue paying the equivalent of public housing operating subsidies to a resident-management-council-owned project while it remains in rental occupancy. But because HUD's near-term privatization policy emphasis is on homeownership rather than revitalization of deteriorating resident-managed developments using non-HUD funds, the department may not be willing to commit to fifteen years of interim operating assistance, the minimum period for which the project financed with federal tax credits must remain in low-income rental use.

Although recent changes in the plans for privatizing Carr Square seem to be bringing it closer to the Kenilworth-Parkside model, final plans for the interim support for Carr Square Village have not yet been made public.

Conclusion

Privatizing public housing is not necessarily a bad idea, but it is very costly, very hard to do right, and has very limited application.

This point was underscored in a recent *Wall Street Journal* article, which pegged the real cost of the Bush administration's empowerment policies—policies that emphasize self-help, free market enterprise, and minimal cost to the government—on a level with the most ambitious welfare state proposals ever dreamed up by liberals.[21]

The article describes the advanced state of disrepair that has befallen the Bromley-Heath complex in Boston. Universally acclaimed as one of the most successful resident-managed public housing complexes in the country, large numbers of units in this 1,000-unit project now lie vacant and unfit for habitation. Neither HUD, the Boston Housing Authority, nor the city have the funds to put Bromley-Heath in sales-ready condition. Nor, after twenty years of resident management, do Bromley-Heath residents have high enough incomes to pay off mortgages without long-term federal subsidies. According to the *Wall Street Journal,* "Impressive strides toward self-sufficiency haven't eradicated a serious unemployment problem at Bromley-Heath. Although tenant-managers have created new job opportunities for some of the 3,000 residents through such ventures as the coin-operated laundry and a van service, the jobless rate [at Bromley-Heath] remains a dismal 81 percent."[22]

In light of all of the evidence thus far, privatizing public housing can only be expected to play a minimal role in the nation's low-income housing policy.

Chapter 6
CONCLUSIONS

B efore additional long-term resources are committed to privatization programs, reevaluation of past success and failure is in order. Based upon the record to date, I would recommend the following policy guidelines:

- HUD should not expand public housing homeownership programs beyond their current demonstration levels:
  - The long-term viability of the dozen or so public housing sales programs created under HUD's national demonstration should be evaluated for at least two more years.
  - The sale of projects to resident management corporations should be limited to Kenilworth-Parkside and Carr Square Village until the costs and benefits of such transfers can be determined on the basis of real, rather than "cooked," data.

- HUD should increase its support for a wide range of creative management initiatives.

- Since there is no empirical evidence that it is cheaper, HUD should stop justifying its support for resident management on the grounds of efficiency and economic development.

- While a revitalized national housing policy should provide for a significant expansion of homeownership opportunities for low-income families, this should not be the centerpiece of the policy.

- It makes more sense to provide opportunities for upwardly mobile families to move out of public housing than it does to sell them their public housing units. First, in the absence of a one-for-one replacement requirement, there is an inadequate supply of high-quality public housing units (the very units that are being sold) for those who cannot afford to live anywhere else. Second, with one-for-one replacement, it is less expensive to move higher-income families of ambition out of public housing into a home of their own than it is to sell a newly renovated public housing unit to its occupant and then to have to replace that unit with another one. Finally, cost considerations aside, the message to the rest of the public housing community is that there is a "way out of the projects" for those who are committed to self-betterment.

• Congress should fully fund the 1990 National Affordable Housing Act programs that would underwrite up to 85 percent of the capital cost of state- and locally designed low- and moderate-income housing initiatives.

• As encouraging as it is to have the federal government back in the housing-production business, with incomes severely lagging housing costs, the centerpiece of a revised national housing policy must be a substantially expanded program of housing vouchers and rental housing certificates.

An Unproven Concept

On the basis of evidence to date, public housing homeownership has not proved itself. HUD's national demonstration of public housing sales, the most thorough empirical study of privatization, uncovered serious problems. These problems include lower-than-anticipated sales; higher-than-anticipated staffing costs and demands; unaffordable and uncontrollable costs in some multifamily conversions; poor-quality rehabilitation; lack of effective protection for some nonbuyers; high contingent liabilities for housing authorities that promised to back up private loans to buyers or co-ops; the absence of replacement housing; and the failure of a number of local programs to get off the ground at all.

Because progress of PHHD sales was only monitored for a year or two after closing, long-term viability—especially affordability—remains in doubt. In Denver, for example, the Upper Lawrence Co-op has had to apply to the housing authority for Section 8 rental assistance. And this probably will not be a unique situation, given the significant number of PHHD buyers who indicated they were having trouble keeping up with the costs of homeownership within a year or so after closing. Should families in HUD's public housing privatization programs routinely require long-term assistance to make it as homeowners, both the concept and the economics of privatization would come into serious question.

Post-sales operating subsidies, which are permitted under the administration's HOPE program, perpetuate the low-income buyer's dependence upon the federal government; resale restrictions severely limit the buyer's opportunity to accumulate capital through homeownership. Taken together, these program requirements blur the distinction between owning and renting to such an extent that privatizing public housing can no longer be promoted as a form of "opportunity capitalism."

Because long-term viability is far from clear, I would recommend that rather than converting the Section 5(h) demonstration into an operating program, HUD should continue monitoring the programs already under way for at least two more years to determine the extent to which current owners are able to make it without long-term subsidies. The same prudence should be exercised with respect to HUD's transfers of public housing projects to resident management corporations under the Section 123 program or its successor programs incorporated into the administration's HOPE initiatives. Not only is there far less empirical data on the economics of these very complicated sales, but much of the existing data is based on unfounded assumptions and overly optimistic projections—and some of it is simply wrong.

For example, HUD, among others, has been touting the results of a 1989 study by Laventhol & Horwath on the feasibility of the Kenilworth-Parkside sale—a study estimating that, over forty years, this sale will represent a long-term savings to the federal government of $26 million.[1] What HUD and other privatization enthusiasts fail to cite from the same report is that "to achieve these results . . . Kenilworth-Parkside must increase tenant rent contributions by 30 percent (adjusted for inflation), while reducing non-utility operating costs by 19 percent over the 5 year conversion period"[2]—something that is not likely to happen. Further, a separate General Accounting Office audit of the proposed sale found that "the project could not support itself beyond year 13."[3] These findings are all the more striking because they apply to what is arguably one of the best-run resident management corporations in the country.

Similar questions have been raised about financial projections on the sale of Carr Square Village to its resident management corporation—specifically the finding that privatization would save the federal government more than $50 million over forty years. According to HUD's inspector general, "The cost savings analysis of private ownership versus public ownership of the Carr Square project, as shown in the August 1989 Carr Square resident homeownership disposition application, was not performed properly."[4] The inspector general found that the cost of replacement housing was not included; that earnings on the project's reserve fund, which accrue to the homeowners, were treated as savings to the federal government; and that the calculations were not in discounted present value terms.

Because plans for the Kenilworth-Parkside and Carr Square transfers are well under way, HUD should consummate these transactions. But until the results of these two transfers are systematically explored, it should not pursue further efforts along these lines. If financing of these two sales continues as described in their respective applications, these two privatization efforts will allow for comparison of the costs and benefits of a HUD-financed transaction (Kenilworth-Parkside) versus a tax credit syndication (Carr Square).

Promoting New Initiatives and Reassessing Justifications

While HUD's renewed emphasis on resident management initiatives in public housing is welcome, this should not be the sole—or even the primary—route to public housing policy reform in the 1990s. For one thing, local conditions are too diverse for a single management model to apply. For another, it leaves other innovative approaches to promoting self-sufficiency—such as Baltimore's Lafayette Court Family Development Center—scratching for funds because they are not resident-management-based. Further, it would discriminate against deserving families who happened to be assigned to housing projects that lack strong resident organizations.

Also, rather than promoting resident management as a cost-saving innovation, as HUD continues to do, resident management should be encouraged because of its potential effectiveness in creating safer, more secure environments, and a higher quality of life for residents who are prepared to take on major responsibilities. Even if resident management costs more, under the proper conditions it might enable HUD to accomplish more of its housing goals than it could otherwise.

An example of the benefits of resident management (and of how HUD's untested assertions about cost savings could undermine a newly planned initiative) is Jack Kemp's recently proposed initiative, Operation Occupancy, intended to rehabilitate some of the 80,000 vacant and abandoned public housing units across the country.

Among other things, Operation Occupancy would simplify the procedures by which public housing authorities apply to HUD for modernization monies, tying award of these funds to the creation of economic opportunities for public housing tenants—including promotion of job training linked to the rehabilitation of public housing (such as construction work). It also would deny nonemergency modernization funds to public housing authorities that are behind schedule in recovering this stock.[5]

This is an excellent idea. Given the $20 billion backlog in meeting public housing modernization needs, this program (if fully funded) could lead to HUD's most ambitious training program in the construction trades for low-income youth. But HUD should not be so naive as to think that creation of such training programs will lead to economies or efficiencies in modernizing public housing. To the contrary, it will slow the pace— which puts Operation Occupancy's promotion of resident involvement at odds with HUD's paramount interest in quickly recovering for reoccupancy most of the 80,000 abandoned public housing units. In short, better will not always be cheaper. But what's wrong with better?

The Bigger Problem: Homeownership Is Only a Partial Solution

HUD's renewed emphasis on extending homeownership opportunities to lower-income families is another welcome addition to our national housing policy. So, too, is HUD's intention to fine-tune its rental assistance programs to promote both residents' self-sufficiency and opportunities for residents to move out of public and assisted housing into homes of their own.

Within this policy framework, it would be appropriate for federal law to authorize housing vouchers to help low-income families buy homes and to end the restrictions that limit use of Section 8 rental certificates solely to co-ops.

But it would be inappropriate to limit the benefits of these rental subsidies to public housing homeownership schemes—which is what HUD's fiscal year 1991 budget does. If, as it appears, the administration's sole interest in broadening the use of rental subsidies to homeownership situations is to replace public housing operating subsidies with housing vouchers, then selling public housing is simply a step toward getting the government out of the housing business.

Paying too large a share of income for housing is now the most widespread housing problem in the country. To place the affordability problem in perspective, it should be noted that, measured in 1989 dollars, the median rent for all poverty-level households without housing subsidies jumped 41 percent between 1974 and 1987, from $255 to $360.[6] This contrasts with a 16 percent increase in all gross rents.[7]

By the time much of the older housing trickles down for low-income renters, it is already substandard and its remaining useful life is limited. In other cases, gentrification pressures generated by both privately and publicly assisted revitalization programs have priced this stock beyond the reach of low-income families. These different market forces have resulted in a substantial decline in the supply of affordable rental housing. There were 3.2 million fewer units renting for less than $300 (measured in 1989 dollars) in 1987 than there were in 1984.[8]

The problem of high housing costs relative to income has been exacerbated by national economic conditions. These adverse economic changes have led to:

- An increase in the number of poor families. Between 1978 and 1985, the number of poor households rose 25 percent, from 10.5 million households to 13.3 million households.

- A decline in the average income of poor families. In 1978, the typical poor family's income was $3,362 below the poverty line. By 1985, the typical poor family's income was $3,999 below the poverty line.
- An increase in the cost of renting a one-bedroom unit to the point where it is beyond the reach of at least one-third of renter households in every single state. It is beyond the reach of more than half of all renter households in six states.[9]

Longtime housing activist Cushing Dolbeare, one of the few to promote a low-income rental assistance entitlement program, has urged the Bush administration to boost federal spending on low-income housing by $30 billion a year, in order to provide housing allowances for low-income households that cannot obtain decent, affordable housing without them.[10] Dolbeare's program would be patterned on Section 8 or voucher programs, and would cover the difference between the amount each household can afford and the monthly cost of housing of the size they need in the area or community where they live. Funds not used for allowances because decent housing is unavailable would, under Dolbeare's plan, be allocated to the local or state agency to acquire, rehabilitate, or build housing that would be permanently reserved for low-income households.

The Congressional Budget Office, which has conducted a systematic analysis of the costs of a universal rental assistance program, estimates that, under such an entitlement, 2.2 million additional very-low-income households could receive benefits at an incremental cost of around $11 billion a year (in 1990 dollars) in new outlays.[11] This is just about equal to the sum of all assisted-housing outlays per year; it is dwarfed (by comparison) by the multibillion-dollar cost to the taxpayers of the savings and loan bailout.

For budgetary reasons, both the administration and Congress will resist any housing program of this size. Given that a substantial portion of the privately held rental stock available to poverty-level families is either being abandoned (to cut losses) or upgraded (in response to more positive market pressures), it is unlikely that affordability problems or homelessness will abate. This means, therefore, that the centerpiece of a revitalized national housing policy must be a significantly expanded rental assistance program.

The Case for Nehemiah: Creating New Low-Cost Housing Stock[12]

The administration has chosen to focus on privatization rather than rental housing assistance. It is doing so through its HOPE initiative, which "basically takes existing program resources and refocuses them around one core theme: increasing opportunities for [assisted] residents to become homeowners."[13] Not only is HOPE's emphasis on home-ownership too narrow to serve as a foundation for a comprehensive low-income housing policy, but also its approach to expanding homeowner-ship opportunities to assisted residents is flawed.

In addition to assisting residents in buying their public housing res-idences, the HOPE initiative calls for the use of Section 8 certificates and vouchers to help low-income tenants buy their investor-owned, sub-sidized housing when low-income use restrictions are about to expire and conversion to market-rate uses would cause wholesale eviction. While, under the circumstances, this is a good idea, there is a more prom-ising way to realize the dream of homeownership for lower-income renters in public housing: sales units should be separate and distinct from the public housing stock.

Take, for example, the federally funded lower-income homeownership demonstration—called the Nehemiah Housing Opportunity Grants program—authorized by the 1987 Housing and Community Development Act.

The demonstration program is based on the highly successful Nehe-miah program (named for the biblical prophet who rebuilt Jerusalem) of a consortium of New York City churches, which built 5,000 single-family homes in a devastated area of East Brooklyn. These homes were built on city-owned land by a nonprofit developer, I. D. Robbins, with the aid of zero-interest construction loans from the consor-tium, tax-exempt financing from the state, and $15,000 deferred-payment second mortgages from the federal Urban Development Action Grant program. Selling for $43,500 (which can be carried by a fam-ily earning $20,000 a year), they are affordable to the higher-income end of the public housing community. According to Robbins, "Based on pub-lished estimates of differential costs, a similar home would be pro-duced in other cities for less, possibly as much as 20 percent less in Baltimore. Much depends on local labor costs and building code requirements."[14]

The Housing and Community Development Act authorized HUD to use $150 million in support of local Nehemiah programs that receive substantial state, local, and private assistance. The goal was to rebuild distressed inner-city neighborhoods around the anchor of Nehemiah communities; to help upwardly mobile tenants of public and other assisted housing to realize their goal of homeownership; and, by free-ing public housing stock, to house low-income families that were on pub-lic housing waiting lists. HUD's participation is in the form of deferred second mortgages.

With the average federal share of a Nehemiah house ($15,000) cost-ing less than a quarter of the federal cost of building a new public housing unit, it makes economic sense to increase the opportunity for families to move out of the "projects." It probably also will be easier to encourage states and localities to contribute to local Nehemiah programs than to share the federal burden of building more public housing. Further, a Nehemiah-type sales program for public housing families with homeownership potential would have the same supply-increasing effects as building a comparable number of new public housing units.

The first round of Nehemiah awards was made in October 1989: fif-teen awards, totaling $18.9 million, to support the construction of more than 1,300 homes for low- and moderate-income buyers across the country. In announcing the awards, HUD Secretary Jack Kemp said: "President Bush and I have made the expansion of homeowner-ship and affordable housing opportunities for low and moderate income families one of our top priorities [and the] Nehemiah Program helps meet that goal."[15]

In May 1990, HUD solicited applications from nonprofit organi-zations for a second, and final, round of Nehemiah housing oppor-tunity grants, this time in the amount of $25.2 million.[16] Despite Jack Kemp's high praise for Nehemiah, the president's very next budget requested no more funds for the program. Ostensibly, this is because, when it comes to homeownership, HOPE could do everything that Nehemiah could do. But since communities are barred from using HOPE funds for new construction, this is not true.

If we are to take at face value the Bush administration's goal to cre-ate a million or more new lower-income homeowners by the end of 1992 without spending a federal dime to create a single new housing unit, then the goal could only be reached through a massive sell-off of the existing federally subsidized rental stock. Thus, we are now able to see the privatization movement for what it really is. Rather than a means of getting the government out of the way (i.e., of promoting greater effi-ciency, consumer choice, and independence), the sale of public hous-ing is, instead, a giant step toward getting the federal government out of the (low-income housing) business and, as such, should be reject-ed as bad public policy.

Looking Ahead

There is an emerging national consensus that homeownership should be an important part, though not the centerpiece, of a revitalized national housing policy.[17] States and localities are prepared to join forces with the federal government to move ahead aggressively on a responsible homeownership agenda. Through the commitment of their own resources to low-income housing, state and local leaders have demonstrated their belief that the delivery of decent housing is as important a public responsibility as is the delivery of clean water or other equally vital municipal services. By both words and deeds, state and local leaders have expressed their belief that low-income homeownership helps build better lives as well as better communities.

But our national housing policy leaders should not confuse consensus on the importance of homeownership with widespread belief in the privatization of public housing. Based on the sorry record of public housing privatization initiatives to date, it is no wonder that the Bush administration has already met stiff opposition to a privatization-based national housing policy.

Early evidence of this resistance may be seen in the fact that, in its May 15 markup of HUD's fiscal year 1992 housing appropriations bill, the House appropriations subcommittee provided no funds at all for the public housing sales portion of HOPE, for which the administration had requested $380 million. When the measure reached the floor, with the threat of a presidential veto of a "HOPE-less" housing appropriations bill hanging over their heads, the House adopted an amendment adding $151 million in 1992 funding for public housing homeownership.[18] While less than half the amount that Jack Kemp indicated was needed, it is likely to be enough to stave off a presidential veto. With the Senate having previously promised modest funding for HOPE, an operational public housing sales program will become a reality in 1992.[19]

Since the initial House appropriations bill contained no money for privatizing public housing, money for HOPE had to be taken from other programs. As if to underscore the point that it makes no sense to sell public housing at a time of tight budgets and so many unmet housing needs, the House ended up taking $151 million in appropriations from a long-standing HUD program that funds the repair and renovation of deteriorated, federally assisted rental housing developments.[20] Thus, a probable consequence of the public housing homeownership program will be a further deterioration in federally assisted rental housing.

I believe that the centerpiece of a revitalized national housing policy must be a major expansion of rental housing assistance, not privatization initiatives. Further, whether applied to a homeownership situation or a rental unit, there must be many more vouchers and certificates in circulation. Yet, the president's fiscal year 1992 housing budget called for an additional allocation of less than 80,000 housing vouchers. At a minimum, the total number of additional vouchers and certificates in the 1992 housing budget should be increased to 200,000. The net cost of adding 120,000 vouchers and certificates would be $700 million in fiscal year 1992 outlays, and $3.5 billion in total multi-year spending (budget authority). The money to fund this increase in low-income housing assistance could come from making modest reductions in the tax breaks currently available to (primarily high-income) homeowners. For example, according to the Congressional Budget Office, limiting mortgage interest deductions for second homes could raise $100 million in revenues in 1991 alone, and a total of $1.3 billion through 1995. [21] Another reasonable approach would be to tax 10 percent of the capital gains on the sale of owner-occupied houses that are now largely exempt from such taxation. According to the Congressional Budget Office, this would yield around $1 billion in revenues in 1991, and $3.4 billion through 1995. [22]

Notes

Chapter 1

1. Drawn from Michael A. Stegman, "Remedies for Homelessness: An Analysis of Potential Housing Policy and Program Responses," The National Conference on Homeless Children and Youth, Washington, D.C., May 1989.

2. U.S. Congress, *HOPE Act of 1990 (Homeownership and Opportunity for People Everywhere,)* section-by-section summary, November 1989; "The Kemp–Bush Plan," *Builder,* July 1990, pp. 60, 62.

3. C. Austin Fitts and J. Kenneth Blackwell, memorandum to Jack Kemp, September 1, 1989.

4. "The Fiscal Year 1991 Budget and Low-Income Housing," special memorandum, Low Income Housing Information Service, Washington, D.C., February 1990, p. 1.

Chapter 2

1. William C. Apgar, "The State of the Nation's Housing: An Update," Joint Center for Housing Studies, Harvard University, Cambridge, Mass., January 1989, p. 3.

2. "The 1989 Low Income Housing Budget," special memorandum, Low Income Housing Information Service, Washington, D.C., April 1988, p. 9.

3. J. M. Gries and J. Ford, *Homeownership, Income and Types of Dwellings,* vol. 4 of the *Report on the President's Conference on Home Building and Homeownership* (Washington, D.C.: National Capital Press, 1927), p. 1.

4. Glen H. Beyer, *Housing and Society* (New York: Macmillan, 1966), p. 249.

5. Lyndon B. Johnson, "The Crisis of the Cities," the President's Message to the Congress on Urban Problems, February 12, 1968.

6. Ann Mariano, "Action Urged to Keep Public Housing Units Available to Poor," *Washington Post,* July 13, 1985.

7. "Special Report '88 Candidates Forum," *Builder,* January 1988, pp. 209–22.

8. U.S. Department of Housing and Urban Development, *The 1978 HUD Survey on the Quality of Community Life, A Data Book,* Louis Harris Associates, New York, 1978, pp. 620–42, 643.

9. Irving Welfeld, *Where We Live: A Social History of American Housing* (New York: Simon and Schuster, 1988), p. 16.

10. Wallace F. Smith, *Housing: Social and Economic Elements* (Los Angeles: University of California Press, 1970), p. 9.

11. Raymond J. Struyk, *Should Government Encourage Homeownership?* (Washington, D.C.: The Urban Institute, 1977).

12. John P. Dean, "The Ghosts of Home Ownership," *Journal of Social Issues* 7, nos. 1 and 2 (special issues: *Social Policy and Social Research*, 1951): 59.

13. Catherine Bauer, "Social Questions in Housing and Community Planning," in ibid. p. 13.

14. Ibid.

15. Eric Carlson, "Policy Implications of Housing Ownership: A Background Paper," Only One Earth Forum, Rene Dubos Society, New York, May 1989, p. 8.

16. Eugene Grigsby et al., cited in J. Kemeny, *The Myth of Homeownership: Private versus Public Choices in Housing Tenure* (London: Routledge & Kegan Paul, 1981), p. 13.

17. Struyk, *Should Government Encourage Homeownership?*, p. 10.

18. William Raspberry, "Kemp at HUD Paving Path out of Dependency," *Raleigh News and Observer*, May 15, 1990.

19. Timothy Barenkov et al., *Privatization and Urban Policy in Britain and the United States* (New York: Oxford University Press, 1989), pp. vii, 1.

20. National Academy of Public Administration, *Privatization: The Challenge to Public Management*, Washington, D.C., 1989, p. 7.

21. E. S. Savas, *Privatization: The Key to Better Government* (Chatham, N.J.: Chatham House, 1987), p. 4.

22. National Academy of Public Administration, *Privatization: The Challenge to Public Management*, p. x.

23. David Fleishaker and Frank Clay, Jr., "Residential Management: A Review of Iroquois Homes" (mimeo), November 1986.

24. Office of the Inspector General, U.S. Department of Housing and Urban Development, *Review of Public Housing Resident Management and Homeownership Programs*, 90-TS-101-003, Washington, D.C., October 24, 1989, p. ii.

25. John D. Donahue, *The Privatization Decision: Public Ends, Private Means* (New York: Basic Books, 1989), p. 215.

26. Janet Rothenberg Pack, "Privatization of Public-Sector Services in Theory and Practice," *Journal of Policy Analysis and Management*, 6, no. 4 (Summer 1987): 532.

27. Savas, *Privatization: The Key to Better Government*, p. 10.

28. Glenn Loury, "Freeing the Inner City Poor," in Mark Lipsitz, ed., *Revitalizing Our Cities: New Approaches to Solving Urban Problems* (Washington, D.C., Fund for an American Renaissance and The National Center for Neighborhood Enterprise, 1986), p. 110.

29. Robert L. Woodson, "A Legacy of Entrepreneurship," in Robert L. Woodson, ed., *On the Road to Economic Freedom: An Agenda for Black Progress* (Washington, D.C.: Regnery Gateway, 1987), p. 1.

30. Loury, "Freeing the Inner City Poor," p. 110.

31. Robert L. Woodson, foreword, in Mark Lipsitz, ed., *Revitalizing Our Cities*, p. xix.

32. Loury, "Freeing the Inner City Poor," p. 110.

33. Woodson, "A Legacy of Entrepreneurship," p. 10.

34. Ibid., p. 19.

35. Stuart M. Butler, *Privatizing Federal Spending: A Strategy to Eliminate the Deficit* (New York: University Books, 1985), p. 40.

36. Office of Policy Development and Research, U.S. Department of Housing and Urban Development, "Issue Paper on the Sale of Public Housing," Washington, D.C., April 6, 1984, p. 5.

37. Mark Kleinman, "New Approaches to Financing Rented Housing in Britain: Where Will Future Supply Come from?" Cambridge University, May 1988, p. 1.

38. Mike Elbro, "U.K. Housing in the 1990s: Challenges, Choices and Change," paper prepared for the National Association of Hosuing and Redevelopment Officials (NAHRO)-Canada Housing Rehabilitation Association (CHRA)-Institute of Housing (IOH) International Conference, "Housing in the '90s: Common Issues," University of Illinois, Urbana-Champaign, October 13–15, 1989, p. 1.

39. Department of Housing and Urban Development, "Issue Paper on the Sale of Public Housing," p. 5.

40. Ray Forrest, "Housing between State and Market," School for Advanced Urban Studies, University of Bristol, September 1988, pp. 16, 19.

41. E. Jay Howenstine, "Converting Public Housing to Individual and Cooperative Ownership: Lessons from Foreign Experience," Office of Policy Development and Research, U.S. Department of Housing and Urban Development, Washington, D.C., August 1983, p. 37.

42. Elbro, "U.K. Housing in the 1990s," p. 3.

43. Forrest, "Housing between State and Market," p. 16.

44. "Public Sector Housing: Future Use, Control, and Management," Institute of Housing, London, June 1987, pp. 7–8.

45. News release, U.K. Department of the Environment, London, November 1988, p. 1.

46. Ibid., p. 2.

47. David N. Butler, "Management of the Public Housing Stock: Renewal Activity and Tenant Involvement," paper prepared for the NAHRO-CHRA-IOH International Conference, "Housing in the '90s: Common Issues," p. 121.

48. Department of Housing and Urban Development, "Issue Paper on the Sale of Public Housing," p. 5.

49. "Section 21 (a) (3) (c) [of the U.S. Housing Act of 1937] should be amended to eliminate the one-for-one replacement provision relating to project buy-outs by RMC's. There simply are not enough housing development funds in HUD's budget to meet the one-for-one housing replacement requirement." Office of the Inspector General, U.S. Department of Housing and Urban Development, Washington, D.C., October 1989, p. 30.

Chapter 3

1. Congressional Budget Office, *Current Housing Problems and Possible Federal Responses*, Washington, D.C., December 1988, pp. 40, 45.

2. Paul A. Leonard, Cushing N. Dolbeare, and Edward B. Lazere, *A Place to Call Home: The Crisis in Housing for the Poor* (Washington, D.C.: Center on Budget and Policy Priorities and the Low Income Housing Information Service, 1989), p. xvii.

3. Fiscal 1991 HUD budget tables, U.S. Department of Housing and Urban Development.

4. J. Kemeny, *The Myth of Homeownership: Private versus Public Choices in Housing Tenure* (London: Routledge & Kegan Paul, 1981), p. 75.

5. "The 1989 Low Income Housing Budget," special memorandum, Low Income Housing Information Service, Washington, D.C., April 1988, p. 9.

6. Leonard et al., *A Place to Call Home*, p. xx.

7. William C. Apgar, "The State of the Nation's Housing: An Update," Joint Center for Housing Studies, Harvard University, Cambridge, Mass., January 1989, p. 10.

8. Walter L. Updegrave, "Race and Money," *Money*, December 1989, p. 152.

9. U.S. Department of Housing and Urban Development, *Housing in the Seventies: A Report of the National Housing Policy Review*, Washington, D.C., 1974, p. 5.

10. Brian Boyer, *Cities Destroyed for Cash: The FHA Scandal at HUD* (Chicago: Follett Publishing Company, 1973), p. 22.

11. Morton Schusheim et al., *Descriptions and Evaluations of Selected Housing Subsidy Programs*, report no. 80-75, Congressional Research Service, Library of Congress, Washington, D.C., March 28, 1978 (updated April 8, 1980), p. 28.

12. Department of Housing and Urban Development, *Housing in the Seventies*, p. 106.

13. Schusheim et al., *Descriptions and Evaluations of Selected Housing Subsidy Programs*, p. 29.

14. Philip N. Brownstein, "Evaluation of the HUD Section 235 Subsidized Housing Program," in *Hearings before a Subcommittee of the Committee on Appropriations: Part 8, Subsidized Housing*, U.S. Congress, House, 95th Cong., 1st sess., 1977, p. 174.

15. Department of Housing and Urban Development, *Housing in the Seventies*, p. 83.

16. Brownstein, "Evaluation of the HUD Section 235 Subsidized Housing Program," p. 179.

17. Schusheim et al., *Descriptions and Evaluations of Selected Housing Subsidy Programs*, p. 29.

18. Boyer, *Cities Destroyed for Cash*, pp. 47–48.

19. Ibid., p. 18.

20. Ibid., p. 119.

21. "Painting Over the Cracks: Section 235, the National Housing Scandal," *Barron's*, December 1975, cited in Brownstein, "Evaluation of the HUD Section 235 Subsidized Housing Program," p. 180.

22. Schusheim et al., *Descriptions and Evaluations of Selected Housing Subsidy Programs*, p. 28.

23. Brownstein, "Evaluation of the HUD Section 235 Subsidized Housing Program," p. 179.

24. The following discussion draws heavily from Michael A. Stegman, William M. Rohe, and Roberto Quercia, "U.S. Experience with the Privatization of Public Housing" (mimeo), Department of City and Regional Planning, University of North Carolina, Chapel Hill, May 1987.

25. U.S. Department of Housing and Urban Development, Office of Inspector General, Region V, "Turnkey III Homeownership Opportunities Program, Chicago Regional Office," audit report, November 1984, p. 4.

26. U.S. Department of Housing and Urban Development, Survey of Section 5(h) and Turnkey III Sales, August 1984.

27. Memorandum from Warren T. Lindquist, assistant secretary for public and Indian housing, to Phil Abrams, undersecretary, U.S. Department of Housing and Urban Development, Washington, D.C., August 3, 1984, p. 2.

28. Department of Housing and Urban Development, "Turnkey III Homeownership Opportunities Program," p. 4.

29. Housing Assistance Council, "A Home of Our Own," report, Washington, D.C., 1988, p. 1.

30. Ibid., p. 5.

31. Ibid., p. 6.

32. Ibid., p. 8.

33. Ibid., p. 2.

34. Henry B. Schechter, "An Analysis of the Section 235 and 236 Programs," Congressional Research Service, Library of Congress, Washington, D.C., May 24, 1973, p. 3.

35. Housing Assistance Council, "A Home of Our Own," p. 2.

36. Brownstein, "Evaluation of the HUD Section 235 Subsidized Housing Program," pp. 180–81.

37. U.S. Department of Housing and Urban Development, *Report to Congress on Housing Counseling*, Washington, D.C., March 1983, pp. 4–5.

38. Ibid., p. 6.

39. The entire letter, written to the chairman of the board of the Jefferson County Home Ownership Program in October 1989, is reproduced with the permission of both the writer and the recipient:

Dear Judge Sloane:

I am writing in regards to the Housing Opportunity Program. My husband, David, and I entered the program in June. At that time we were heavily in debt and didn't know which way to turn. To make matters worse my husband and I, with our two children, were living with my parents. We had been forced to move in with them three years before due to a series of bad luck...

The very first time we met with Linda Wilcox [the executive director], we felt as though the program had been tailor made for us. Naturally, we were pleased with the prospect of owning our own home, but more importantly, we would learn lifetime lessons in handling our finances. We found immediately that we had not been utilizing my husband's paycheck at all, and had not been utilizing mine to its fullest extent. We now have a budget that we follow, we pay our bills on time, and have our priorities straight. We have paid off all but two of our bills in just five months. One particular lesson has been very difficult to learn, and that is to say "no" when our children ask for something. Naturally, they have everything they need. However, we have always tried to give them everything they wanted as well. Now, they also are learning the value of money. We hope this will enable them to avoid the same mistakes we have made.

If everything continues to go well, we will be able to pay off the remaining two bills and buy a home in 1990. I cannot give enough credit to Linda Wilcox and the Housing Opportunity Program. Our lives have been turned around and we can look forward to the future.

Sincerely, Lisa Minzenberger

40. Housing Assistance Council, "A Home of Our Own," p. 18.

41. Ibid.

42. U.S. Department of Housing and Urban Development, "Home-ownership Opportunities under the Section 8 Program," memorandum, Washington, D.C., May 1982, p. 3.

43. Ibid.

44. Michael A. Stegman, "The Case for Low-Income Homeownership," paper prepared for presentation at a conference of the National Association of Housing and Redevelopment Officials (NAHRO), San Antonio, July 29, 1990, p. 10.

45. This section draws heavily on Michael A. Stegman, "The Role of Public Housing in a Revitalized National Low Income Housing Policy," in Denise DiPasquale and Langley C. Keyes, eds., *Building Foundations: Housing and Federal Policy* (Philadelphia: University of Pennsylvania Press, 1990), pp. 336–64.

46. Section 6(a), U.S. Housing Act of 1937, as amended.

47. Council of Large Public Housing Authorities, *Public Housing Today*, report, Boston, September 1986, pp. 13, 15.

48. NAHRO, *The Many Faces of Public Housing* (Washington, D.C.: National Association of Housing and Redevelopment Officials, 1990), p. 2.

49. Wayne Sherwood and Elizabeth March, "Operating Subsidies for

Public Housing: Problems and Options," working paper, Citizens Housing and Planning Association, Boston, August 1983, p. 3.

50. Ibid.

51. U.S. Congress, House, Committee on Banking, Finance and Urban Affairs, Subcommittee on Housing and Community Development, *Housing, Community Development and Homeless Prevention Act of 1987*, report to Accompany HR-4, report 100-122, June 1987, p. 20.

Chapter 4

1. William Raspberry, "Kemp at HUD Paving Path out of Dependency," *Raleigh News and Observer*, May 15, 1990, p. 9A.

2. The data contained in this chapter are from William M. Rohe and Michael A. Stegman, *Public Housing Homeownership Demonstration Assessment*, prepared for the U.S. Department of Housing and Urban Development, Washington, D.C., contract HC-5774, April 1990.

3. Office of Policy Development Research, U.S. Department of Housing and Urban Development, "The Financial Status of Scattered-Site Public Housing," unpublished report, Washington, D.C., October 1985, pp. 1–2.

4. *An Actuarial Review of the Federal Housing Administration's Mutual Mortgage Insurance Fund*, Price Waterhouse, Washington, D.C., June 6, 1990.

5. Technically, the national Federal Housing Administration data present "claim rates" rather than foreclosure rates because some loan failures end up with the borrower transferring his deed to the lender in lieu of foreclosure. From the standpoint of the borrower, however, the end result is the same—loss of his home.

6. *An Actuarial Review of the Federal Housing Administration's Mutual Mortgage Insurance Fund*, p. 12.

7. Ibid, p. 13.

8. William M. Rohe and Michael A. Stegman, *An Evaluation of the Public Housing Homeownership Demonstration*, draft final report, U.S. Department of Housing and Urban Development, Washington, D.C., December 1989, pp. 163–64.

9. *An Actuarial Review of the Federal Hosing Administration's Mutual Mortgage Insurance Fund*, p. 11.

10. Ibid., p. 10.

11. Ibid.

12. William Raspberry, "Kemp at HUD Paving Path out of Dependency," *Raleigh News and Observer*, May 15, 1990, p. 9A.

13. Bureau of National Affairs, *Housing and Development Reporter* 18, no. 24 (October 29, 1990): 519.

14. J. Michael Dorsey, assistant secretary of housing, letter to Senator William Proxmire, December 11, 1986, p. 1.

15. Ibid., p. 3.

16. David Caprara and Bill Alexander, *Empowering Residents of Public Housing* (Washington, D.C.: National Center for Neighborhood Enterprise, 1989), p. 32.

17. Office of the Inspector General, U.S. Department of Housing and Urban Development, *Review of Public Housing Resident Management and Homeownership Programs*, 90-TS-101-003,Washington, D.C., October 24, 1989, p. 70.

18. Manpower Development Research Corporation, *Final Report of the National Tenant Management Demonstration*, Washington, D.C., May 1980, p. 64.

19. U.S. Department of Housing and Urban Development notice, "Processing of Applications for Fiscal Year (FY) 1989 Funds for Public Housing Resident Management," *Public and Indian Housing* 89-7, Washington, D.C., February 16, 1989

20. U.S. Department of Housing and Urban Development regulation, "Tenant Participation and Management," 24CFR964, December 8, 1986, p. l9.

21. General Accounting Office, *Public Housing: Planned Kenilworth-Parkside Sale Raises Issues for Future Transactions*, GAO/RCED-90-26, Washington, D.C., December 1989, p. 29.

22. Editorial, *Washington Times*, October 17, 1988.

23. Robert L. Woodson, ed., *On the Road to Economic Freedom: An Agenda for Black Progress* (Washington, D.C.: Regnery Gateway, 1987), p. 24.

24. Caprara and Alexander, *Empowering Residents of Public Housing*, p. 1.

25. David Fleishaker and Frank Clay, Jr., "Resident Management: A Review of Iroquois Homes," 1986.

26. Ibid., p. 7.

27. Ibid.

28. Manpower Development Research Corporation, *Final Report of the National Tenant Management Demonstration*, Washington, D.C., May 1980, p. xviii.

29. Ibid., pp.xviii–xix.

30. Ibid., pp. xxii–xxiii.

31. Department of Housing and Urban Development, *Review of Public Housing Resident Management and Homeownership Programs*, pp. 5–6.

32. Ibid., p. 5.

33. Ibid., pp. 44–48.

34. Ibid., p. 48.

35. Ibid., p. 29.

36. Ibid.

37. Robert L. Woodson, "Final Report and Evaluation of the Public Housing Resident Management Program, a Three Year Demonstration," The Amoco Foundation, Chicago, September 15, 1988, p. 4.

38. Ibid., p. 1.

39. Cavanaugh is quoted in David Osborne, "They Can't Stop Us Now," *The Washington Post Magazine*, July 30, 1989, p. 17.

40. Housing and Community Development Act of 1987.

41. U.S. Department of Housing and Urban Development, Public Housing Homeownership Notice, *Federal Register* 53, no. 213 (November 3, 1988): 44558.

42. General Accounting Office, *Planned Kenilworth-Parkside Sale Raises Issues for Future Transactions*, p. 46.

43. Ibid.

44. Department of Housing and Urban Development, *Review of Public Housing Resident Management and Homeownership Programs*.

45. Lafayette Court Family Development Center fact sheet, Baltimore, n.d.

46. Letter from Ann B. Shlay, principal investigator, Johns Hopkins University, to John Lanigan, program officer, The Ford Foundation, August 1989.

47. Housing Authority of the City of Charlotte, "Gateway Housing: A Transitional Housing Demonstration Program of the Housing Authority of the City of Charlotte, North Carolina," unpublished report, revised October 1988, p. 6.

48. Ibid., p. 1.

49. Ibid., pp. 12–13.

Chapter 5

1. Letter dated February 15, 1989, to Mr. John P. Helm, general manager of the Denver Housing Authority, from Kenneth J. Beirne, assistant secretary for policy development and research, U.S. Department of Housing and Urban Development.

2. William M. Rohe and Michael A. Stegman, *Public Housing Homeownership Demonstration Assessment, Case Studies* (Washington, D.C.: U.S. Department of Housing and Urban Development, 1990), p. 166.

3. General Accounting Office, *Public Housing: Planned Kenilworth-Parkside Sale Raises Issues for Future Transactions*, GAO/RCED-90-26, Washington, D.C., December 1989, p. 16.

4. Ibid., p. 34.

5. Ibid., p. 18.

6. Office of the Inspector General, U.S. Department of Housing and Urban Development, *Review of Public Housing Resident Management and Homeownership Programs*, 90-TS-101-003, Washington, D.C., October 24, 1989, p. 64.

7. Rohe and Stegman, *Public Housing Homeownership Demonstration Assessment, Case Studies*, pp. 150–61.

8. Ibid., pp. 27–28; Alan Gottlieb, "DHA Pilot Projects Riddled with Woes," *Denver Post*, January 11, 1991, p. 1B.

9. General Accounting Office, *Planned Kenilworth-Parkside Sale Raises Issues for Future Transactions*, p. 50.

10. Ibid., p. 80.

11. Timothy Noah, "Bush 'Empowerment' Self-Help Plans for the Poor Could Prove as Costly as Any Proposal by Liberals," *Wall Street Journal*, January 30, 1991, p. A12.

12. General Accounting Office, *Planned Kenilworth-Parkside Sale Raises Issues for Future Transactions*, p. 23.

13. Ibid., p. 23.

14. Ibid., p. 25.

15. Ibid., p. 3.

16. U.S. Congress, Senate, Committee on Banking, Housing, and Urban Affairs, Subcommittee on Housing and Urban Affairs, draft, section 651, *Homeownership Opportunities for Residents of Public Housing*, 101st Cong., 2d sess., 1989.

17. General Accounting Office, *Planned Kenilworth-Parkside Sale Raises Issues for Future Transactions*, p. 26.

18. Department of Housing and Urban Development, *Review of Public Housing Resident Management and Homeownership Programs*, p. 34.

19. Ibid., p. 37.

20. Ibid., p. 38.

21. Noah, "Bush 'Empowerment' Self-Help for the Poor," p. A12.

22. Ibid.

Chapter 6

1. Laventhol & Horwath, *Economic and Financial Study of Kenilworth-Parkside*, conducted on behalf of the National Center for Neighborhood Enterprise, Washington, D.C., September 1, 1989, pp. 2–3.

2. Ibid., p. 2.

3. General Accounting Office, *Public Housing: Planned Kenilworth-Parkside Sale Raises Issues for Future Transactions*, GAO/RCED-90-26, Washington, D.C., December 1989, p. 50.

4. Office of the Inspector General, U.S. Department of Housing and Urban Development, *Review of Public Housing Resident Management and Homeownership Programs*, 90-TS-101-003, Washington, D.C., October 24, 1989, p. 36.

5. *Housing Development Reporter* 17, no. 39 (February 19, 1990): 753.

6. Joint Center for Housing Studies, *The State of the Nation's Housing, 1990* (Cambridge, Mass.: Harvard University Press, 1990), p. 21.

7. Ibid.

8. Ibid., p. 30.

9. Cushing Dolbeare, *Out of Reach: Why Everyday People Can't Find Affordable Housing*, Low Income Housing Information Service, Washington, D.C., September 1989, p. 3.

10. Ibid.

11. Congressional Budget Office, *Current Housing Problems and Possible Federal Responses*, Washington, D.C., December 1988, p. 105.

12. This section draws from Michael A. Stegman, "The Role of Public Housing in a Revitalized National Housing Policy," in Denise DiPasquale and Langley C. Keyes, eds., *Building Foundations: Housing and Federal Policy* (Philadelphia: University of Pennsylvania Press, 1990).

13. "The Fiscal Year 1991 Budget and Low-Income Housing," special memorandum, Low Income Housing Information Service, Washington, D.C., February 1990, p. 1.

14. I. D. Robbins, "Affordable Single-Family Housing Grows in Brooklyn," *Real Estate Journal*, Winter 1987, p. 50.

15. U.S. Department of Housing and Urban Development, news release, October 13, 1989.

16. *Housing and Development Reporter* 18, no. 2 (May 28, 1990): 19.

17. See, for example, summaries of some of the many state and local home-ownership assistance programs that have been created since the federal retreat in Federal National Mortgage Association, *Fannie Mae's Low- and Moderate-Income Housing Initiatives*, Washington, D.C., March 1990, pp. 31–120.

18. *Housing Development Reporter* 19, no. 2 (May 27, 1991): 1.

19. In arguing for full funding of HOPE at a Senate hearing on June 5, 1991, Jack Kemp said that "the Administration is not ready to accept another [public housing homeownership] demonstration." *Housing and Development Reporter* 19, no. 4 (June 10, 1991): 83.

20. Money for the public housing sales program came from the flexible subsidy program for troubled multifamily projects.

21. Congressional Budget Office, *Reducing the Deficit: Spending and Revenue Options*, Washington, D.C., February 1990, p. 357.

22. "The tax on the capital gain from the sale of a principal residence is deferred if the seller purchases another home of at least equal value within two years. If the gain does not become taxable during the homeowner's lifetime, the gain is never taxed at all." Further, taxpayers age fifty-five and over are allowed one opportunity to exclude up to $125,000 of gain from a home sale even if another home of equal or greater value is not purchased within two years. Congressional Budget Office, *Reducing the Deficit*, p. 361.

Index